SHEFFIELD WEDNESDAY
On This Day

SHEFFIELD WEDNESDAY
On This Day

*History, Facts & Figures
from Every Day of the Year*

JASON DICKINSON

SHEFFIELD WEDNESDAY
On This Day

History, Facts & Figures from Every Day of the Year

All statistics, facts and figures are correct as of 1st August 2009

© Jason Dickinson

Jason Dickinson has asserted his rights in accordance with the Copyright, Designs and Patents Act 1988 to be identified as the author of this work.

Published By:
Pitch Publishing (Brighton) Ltd
A2 Yeoman Gate
Yeoman Way
Durrington
BN13 3QZ

Email: info@pitchpublishing.co.uk
Web: www.pitchpublishing.co.uk

First published 2009

A catalogue record for this book is available from the British Library.

10-digit ISBN: 1-9054115-6-1
13-digit ISBN: 978-1-9054115-6-6

Printed and bound in India by Replika Press Pvt. Ltd.

Dedicated to my wife Michelle,
whose love and patience
helped me compile this book.

FOREWORD BY DAVID HIRST

My career at Sheffield Wednesday began on the day I was called into the manager's office at Barnsley and was told to report to Hillsborough, as I had been sold to the Owls! Ironically, a few days earlier I had told a friend that I would not join rivals Wednesday for a "gold pig".

My father and I duly met Howard Wilkinson and I signed on the dotted line, starting an association with Wednesday that would provide the best days of my playing career. Despite scoring on my home debut I was on the fringes of the first team during my early months at Hillsborough, my fitness not being sufficient for Wilkinson, but I slowly started to become a first team regular as Peter Eustace, and then Ron Atkinson, took charge at Hillsborough.

The revolution in both playing style and ambition under 'Big Ron' was marked and Atkinson was the best manager I would play under. The terrific promotion and cup-winning season of 1990/91 ended on a real high as after representing England in a 'B' international, I was asked by Graham Taylor if I had any plans for the summer. After saying I had none he said "that's good" because he wanted me to join England's tour of Australasia! I scored against New Zealand in my second game and then appeared against France at Wembley later in the year.

That season also saw me link up with Paul Williams and we became an irresistible double act – I always promised him that if he kept setting up goals for me I would mention his name occasionally on *Match of the Day*! The side of the early 1990s was the best team I played in – my goal in the 1993 FA Cup final the most memorable moment of my career – although my desire to get back in the team after being injured probably counted against my fitness in the long run.

My career at Wednesday came to a close after a clash of personalities with Owls manager David Pleat, resulting in a move to Southampton. Ironically, a few weeks after I left, the club sacked Pleat and if I'd known that in advance it's likely I would have ended my playing days at Hillsborough. My son has recently signed to the Owls' academy and I still have a great affinity with the club, being a regular on a match day at Hillsborough.

To all Wednesday fans around the globe, you have a great club, with a great history, which is now starting to take strides to reclaim their former glories. Enjoy the read.

David Hirst, Sheffield Wednesday 1986-1997
128 goals in 358 games, 3 England caps

INTRODUCTION

Sheffield Wednesday On This Day chronicles every facet of the club's long and rich history, from their formation back in 1867 to present-day attempts to reclaim a Premiership place. Packed with fascinating facts, figures and trivia this book will delight all those fans who love their club: Sheffield Wednesday.

Written in a unique diary format, the book starts on the first day of the year and follows the club's ups and downs on every subsequent day, all the way through to New Year's Eve. January traditionally signifies the start of the FA Cup trail while in Wednesday's case, spring usually means some kind of championship, promotion or relegation battle! The quieter summer months tend to be dominated by transfer activity while pre-season games all over the world precede the optimistic start to every new season.

Along the way *On This Day* covers all the major matches in the Owls' history and details all the major players – and some not so famous – that have helped shape the club we know today. The book also focuses on the rather off-beat stories as well – see if you can spot the day when a male streaker invaded the Hillsborough pitch, wearing only socks, shoes and a pair of spectacles!

Jason Dickinson, 2009

ACKNOWLEDGEMENTS

I would like to express my thanks to all those at Pitch Publishing, most notably Dan Tester who has guided me through the various stages that eventually result in a book hitting the shelves. A big thank you to David Hirst for penning the foreword and also thanks to Sheffield Wednesday for giving their permission for the official badge to adorn the cover of this publication and particularly to Trevor Braithwait, Colin Wood and Sue Evans at the club for their help.

Finally thanks to friends, and fellow Wednesday fans, Mick Grayson, Pete Law, Stuart Laver and Roger Strain who have searched their memory banks for the more offbeat events in the Owls' history.

SHEFFIELD WEDNESDAY
On This Day

JANUARY

WEDNESDAY 1st JANUARY 1913

In a thrilling game at Hillsborough, Wednesday recovered from being three goals in arrears after 75 minutes to force a 3-3 draw. A 40,000-strong crowd saw David McLean score twice and Sam Kirkman once – all the goals being scored inside a ten-minute period.

TUESDAY 1st JANUARY 1929

A new record crowd for a league game at Hillsborough of 57,143 packed into the ground to see First Division leaders Wednesday face neighbours Huddersfield Town. The Terriers went ahead after 64 minutes but the Owls retained first position after a late goal from Bob Gregg secured a 1-1 draw.

WEDNESDAY 1st JANUARY 1930

The biggest game in the top division saw Wednesday travel to Manchester City where almost 56,000 fans watched as the Owls surged into a 3-0 lead, thanks to goals from Ellis Rimmer, Jack Allen and Jimmy Seed. However, the home team stormed back to cut the deficit to a single goal before future Wednesday manager, Jimmy McMullan, grabbed an 83rd-minute equaliser as the teams shared six goals. The point left Wednesday top of the division and on course for back-to-back league titles.

SATURDAY 1st JANUARY 1966

After breaking the 500-game barrier for Wednesday and winning England B and under-23 honours, Alan Finney played his final game for the club – a 3-0 defeat to Leeds United at Elland Road.

WEDNESDAY 1st JANUARY 1985

Newly promoted Wednesday travelled to Old Trafford where the majority of the 47,638 crowd were shocked when Imre Varadi put the away side ahead after just 13 minutes. United equalised through Mark Hughes after 63 minutes, and eight minutes later the points look set to stay with the home side when Martin Hodge brought down Hughes inside the area to concede a penalty. However, the Owls custodian saved Gordon Strachan's spot kick and a Varadi header duly secured a famous 2-1 win to lift Wednesday into fifth place, to the delight of the large travelling band of Owls fans.

SUNDAY 1st JANUARY 2006

On the first day of the January transfer window, Paul Sturrock completed a double signing as Marcus Tudgay arrived from Derby County on loan, along with Deon Burton, the latter signing from Rotherham United for a reputed £110,000 fee. Tudgay – who signed a permanent deal four days later – netted on his debut on the following day while Jamaican international Burton scored 26 goals in 124 games for the club before moving on a free transfer to Charlton Athletic in January 2009.

MONDAY 2nd JANUARY 1893

Two goals from 'the Olive Grove flyer' Fred Spiksley helped Wednesday to a 6-0 win over West Bromwich Albion in a top flight fixture at Olive Grove. Also on target were Harry Brandon, Alec Brady, Alex Rowan and 'Sparrow' Brown.

WEDNESDAY 2nd JANUARY 1907

Left-winger Ellis James Rimmer was born in Birkenhead and would become one half of the wing partnership that powered Wednesday to success during the inter-war years. With Mark Hooper on the opposite wing, the pair scored an astonishing 275 goals, with Rimmer notching 140 in 417 games.

SATURDAY 2nd JANUARY 1971

Long-serving defender Gerry Young played his final game as Wednesday lost 4-1 to Tottenham Hotspur in an FA Cup game at White Hart Lane. A David Sunley goal had equalised a Martin Peters strike but goals from Alan Gilzean (2) and Alan Mullery knocked the Owls out of the competition.

SATURDAY 3rd JANUARY 1880

Wednesday player H. Moss became the first recorded substitute in the club's history after replacing William Clegg, in the 3-0 defeat to Scottish club Vale of Leven in a friendly played at Sheaf House.

SATURDAY 3rd JANUARY 1914

On a calamitous afternoon at Hillsborough, the Owls were beaten 6-2 by Burnley – a result that stood until January 1992 as the club's heaviest home loss.

SATURDAY 3RD JANUARY 1981

A gangly youngster by the name of Chris Waddle scored both goals for Newcastle United as Wednesday lost 2-1 at St. James' Park, in the FA Cup third round.

MONDAY 3RD JANUARY 1983

In front of just 11,799 fans, the Owls and Charlton Athletic served up a nine-goal extravaganza with the Londoners surging into a 3-1 lead after Andy McCulloch had scored for Wednesday after just six minutes. With Charlton's star player, Danish international Allan Simonsen, on top form defeat looked certain but Gary Bannister and McCulloch proceeded to level the scores after 61 minutes. However, a minute later it was 4-3 to Charlton after an error from Bob Bolder. The scoring did not end there, though, as an own goal levelled matters again before a fifth goal in fifteen minutes, from Mick Lyons, sealed a 5-4 win for Wednesday.

SATURDAY 3RD JANUARY 1987

A below strength Wednesday side were beaten 6-1 by Leicester City at Filbert Street with Steve Moran netting three for the home side. The Owls gave debuts to defender Kenny Brannigan and winger David Tomlinson but, for both, it was their only taste of first team football with Wednesday.

SATURDAY 4TH JANUARY 1896

The club's reserve side went goal crazy at Olive Grove as Eckington Works were beaten 18-0 in a Sheffield Challenge Cup fixture. William Gooing led the way with five goals to his name while Albert Kaye also bagged a treble.

SATURDAY 4TH JANUARY 1964

Wednesday were knocked out of the FA Cup at Third Division Newport County, losing 3-2 despite having led twice, in front of 12,342 at Somerton Park.

SATURDAY 4TH JANUARY 1997

The Owls put seven past Hillsborough opponents Grimsby Town in an FA Cup third round tie. Andy Booth and Richie Humphreys led the way with two goals each in front of a 20,590 crowd.

SATURDAY 5TH JANUARY 1946

Eighteen-year-old attacker Redfern Froggatt made his debut for Wednesday as they were held 0-0 at Mansfield Town in the first leg of a third round FA Cup tie.

SATURDAY 5TH JANUARY 1952

The ground record for a league game was set on this day as a crowd of 65,384 packed into Hillsborough to watch the Second Division derby against the Blades. The almost inevitable goal from Derek Dooley made the score 1-1 at the break but the Blades quickly regained the lead and Wednesday's hopes were dashed when Redfern Froggatt saw his penalty kick saved. United scored again after 80 minutes to complete a 3-1 win.

SATURDAY 6TH JANUARY 1900

Scotsman Harry Millar became the first Wednesday player to score four times in a league fixture as Gainsborough Trinity were beaten 5-1 at Owlerton in a Second Division game. Millar would net 16 times in 34 games for Wednesday but left in 1901 after having earlier been suspended without pay for not attending training!

FRIDAY 6TH JANUARY 1933

Tom McAnearney was born in Lochee, Dundee. The half-back would give the Owls terrific service during 14 years at Hillsborough, appearing in 382 games and scoring 22 times.

SATURDAY 6TH JANUARY 1934

Wednesday drew 1-1 at Arsenal in a First Division encounter but the game was played under a cloud as on the morning of the match the Gunners' legendary manager, Herbert Chapman, died. The players wore black armbands, a bugler played the *Last Post* and a minute's silence preceded the game.

WEDNESDAY 6TH JANUARY 1937

Owls fans were not happy in the slightest when FA Cup-winning captain Ron Starling was sold to Aston Villa for a club record £6,900. The sale came just 24 hours after Wednesday had refused a club record bid from Arsenal for the signature of Jackie Robinson.

SATURDAY 6TH JANUARY 1979

Hundreds of Owls fans helped to clear the snow off the Hillsborough pitch so the FA Cup match with First Division Arsenal could go ahead. The hard work paid off as Wednesday held the Gunners to a 1-1 draw (Jeff Johnson) with visiting goalkeeper Pat Jennings being mercilessly pelted by snowballs throughout the cup-tie!

SATURDAY 7TH JANUARY 1989

Despite Fourth Division opponents Torquay United taking the lead after just three minutes, the Owls hit back to win 5-1 in front of just 11,384 at Hillsborough. The victory was Peter Eustace's only win at home as Owls boss during a calamitous 109 days in charge.

SATURDAY 7TH JANUARY 1995

The Owls met basement club Gillingham in the FA Cup and were 2-0 ahead when Kevin Pressman was sent off after conceding a penalty. He was replaced by rookie keeper Lance Key – his only appearance for the club – but despite failing to stop the resultant spot kick he performed heroics as Wednesday held on to win 2-1 in Kent.

WEDNESDAY 7TH JANUARY 2009

Lifelong Wednesdayite Lee Strafford was appointed as the club's 14th chairman, filling the void left by Dave Allen's resignation back in November 2007. Also appointed on the same day was Nick Parker, as the Owls' new chief executive.

SATURDAY 8TH JANUARY 1887

With only ten men, Wednesday found themselves 8-0 in arrears at half-time in a friendly at Lancashire club, Halliwell. The home side doubled their score in the second half to win 16-0 – the worst recorded defeat in any first team fixture for Wednesday.

SATURDAY 8TH JANUARY 1898

In the absence of Ambrose Langley, the Owls gave a debut to Willie Layton in the First Division game at Everton. Wednesday lost 1-0. Layton would only play senior football for the Owls, appearing in 361 games before retiring in 1910.

SATURDAY 8TH JANUARY 1938

The Owls met Burnley in an FA Cup tie at Hillsborough with new manager Jimmy McMullan in charge for the first time after moving from Notts County. The new boss needed a last minute equaliser from Harry Millership to force a replay while the crowd were entertained at half-time when a young Burnley supporter ran with a ball from one end of the pitch to the other, only to fire against a post from a few inches out. Rumours that he was signed by Wednesday soon after proved unfounded!

SATURDAY 8TH JANUARY 1983

Wednesday's Gary Megson and Southend United full-back Micky Stead were both sent off in the second half of a hard fought 0-0 FA Cup game at Roots Hall.

TUESDAY 8TH JANUARY 2002

In front of a 30,883 Hillsborough crowd, the Owls lost 2-1 to Premiership Blackburn Rovers in the first leg of the League Cup semi-final. The Lancashire side scored twice in the first half, through Craig Hignett and Andy Cole, before Efan Ekoku's 51st-minute strike gave Wednesday hope for the second leg.

MONDAY 9TH JANUARY 1922

The club mourned the death of 'A' team player George Pennington who died of pneumonia

TUESDAY 9TH JANUARY 1979

The Owls were just a minute away from being FA Cup giant-killers as a last gasp Liam Brady goal equalised a Roger Wylde strike in the 44th minute of the 1-1 draw at Highbury. A crowd of 37,987 saw the Owls force a third match, after extra time could not separate the teams.

SATURDAY 10TH JANUARY 1925

A brace from Harold Hill secured a 2-0 FA Cup win over fellow Second Division side Manchester United at Hillsborough. Before the tie the crowd watched the somewhat bizarre sight of United's mascot – a one-legged man dressed in red and white hoops – hopping around the pitch!

SATURDAY 10TH JANUARY 1931

Redheugh Park, home of Division Three (North) club Gateshead, was packed to see the visit of league champions Wednesday in the FA Cup. The Owls raced into a 2-0 lead after just six minutes thanks to goals from Mark Hooper and Jack Allen. A penalty kick from Jack Ball extended that lead and although Gateshead pulled the score back to 3-2, the Owls raced away to win 6-2.

SATURDAY 11TH JANUARY 1908

On a frozen Newmarket Road pitch the Owls tumbled out of the FA Cup at the first round stage, losing 2-0 at Southern League Norwich City. The holders went out to a goal in each half in front of a sell out 10,326 crowd which generated receipts of just over £668.

SATURDAY 11TH JANUARY 1936

A decision by Crewe Alexandra to double their prices, for their FA Cup tie against Wednesday, backfired as the smallest crowd in the country, 9,755, watched the sides draw 1-1 with Jack Surtees equalising for the Owls to force a replay.

TUESDAY 11TH JANUARY 1994

A rare long range strike from Mark Bright sent the Owls through to the semi-finals of the League Cup as they won 2-1 at Wimbledon.

SATURDAY 11TH JANUARY 2003

In a Hillsborough thriller, Wednesday recovered from a two-goal half-time deficit to beat Reading 3-2. The comeback was inspired by the enigmatic Gerald Sibon who equalised after 68 minutes in his final game in an Owls shirt. He joined Dutch side Heerenveen four days later, after 43 goals in 150 games for Wednesday.

SATURDAY 12TH JANUARY 1907

Wednesday opened their FA Cup campaign with a 3-2 win over Wolves at Owlerton. In front of 21,938 fans, Wednesday came back from two goals behind to net three times in just twelve minutes, in the second period, to secure a place in the next round.

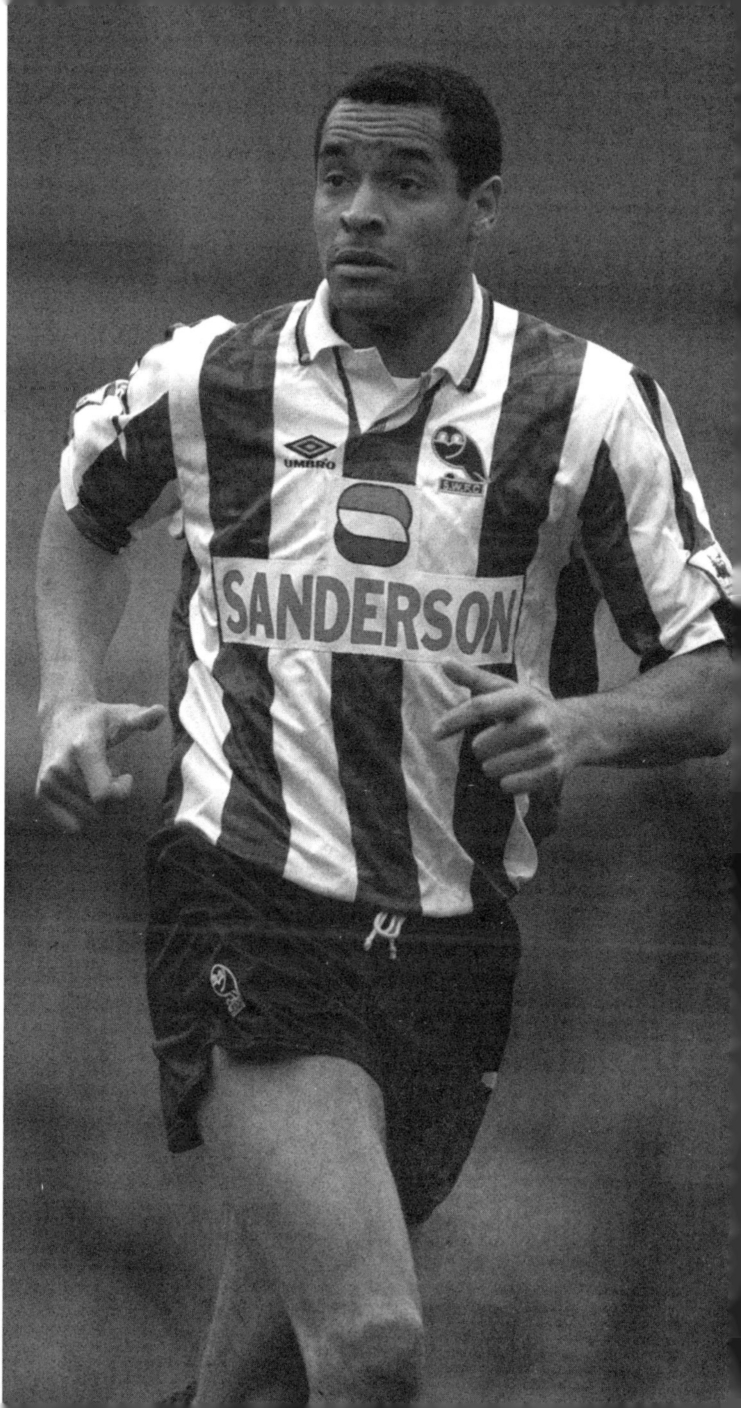

MARK BRIGHT, SCORER OF THE LEAGUE CUP WINNER AT WIMBLEDON

SATURDAY 12TH JANUARY 1924

Three penalties were awarded at Hillsborough in the FA Cup tie versus Leicester City. Wednesday forward Sid Binks missed twice but netted the rebound from his first miss and Wednesday, 4-0 ahead at half-time, won 4-1.

SATURDAY 12TH JANUARY 1935

Wednesday started their FA Cup campaign on a Hillsborough pitch frozen with compacted snow! The home side adapted better to conditions than visitors Oldham Athletic, winning 3-1 in front of 26,662.

SATURDAY 12TH JANUARY 1939

The gates were closed at The Huish as a record 14,359 crowd squeezed in for the FA Cup tie between non-league Yeovil & Petters United and Wednesday. The 300 fans locked out missed an end-to-end tie, which the Owls won 2-1 through Dai Lewis and Charlie Napier.

SUNDAY 12TH JANUARY 1992

The Owls were humbled on national TV as Yorkshire rivals Leeds United romped to a 6-1 win at Hillsborough, against a Wednesday side depleted by injuries and illness.

WEDNESDAY 13TH JANUARY 1954

In a fierce FA Cup replay at Bramall Lane, the referee spoke to both captains about the numerous fouls. The game was tied at 1-1 after Wednesday keeper Brian Ryalls had saved a ninth-minute penalty and Alan Finney had equalised after 52 minutes. However, Vin Kenny then became the first Wednesday player to be sent off in post-war football but despite their numerical disadvantage Wednesday secured a famous win with George Davies and Jackie Sewell finding the target.

WEDNESDAY 13TH JANUARY 1988

Wednesday led 1-0 through a Lee Chapman header in the FA Cup third round replay at Goodison Park but Everton hit back to take the tie into extra time and a third match.

SATURDAY 14TH JANUARY 1905

A hat-trick from Jimmy Stewart helped to beat visitors Bury 4-0 in a top flight game with Tom Brittleton making his Wednesday debut at inside-right.

SATURDAY 14TH JANUARY 1984

In blizzard conditions, Wednesday thrashed Swansea City 6-1 at Hillsborough to confirm their position as Second Division leaders. Goals from Mick Lyons, John Pearson, Gary Megson, Pat Heard, Imre Varadi and an own goal from Swans player-manager John Toshack completed the best win of the season.

WEDNESDAY 14TH JANUARY 1998

Goalkeeper Kevin Pressman was the hero of the FA Cup third round replay at Hillsborough against Watford. After the tie had finished 0-0 he saved from a Micah Hyde penalty in the shoot out and blasted home the winner as Wednesday progressed 5-3 on penalties.

SATURDAY 15TH JANUARY 1921

Wednesday lost 1-0 at Port Vale in a game that saw a chaotic finish to the first half as the referee realised he had blown for time after just 42 minutes. He then had to usher off the marching band so the teams could play the remaining three minutes!

SATURDAY 15TH JANUARY 2005

The Owls drew 1-1 at Bournemouth thanks to an injury time equaliser from Paul Heckingbottom. The game also marked the last appearance of loan star Kenwyne Jones who returned to Southampton after scoring seven times in seven games.

THURSDAY 16TH JANUARY 1913

In an FA Cup first round tie at Hillsborough, Grimsby Town were beaten 5-1 with David McLean netting four goals in a game for the second time in his Wednesday career. The 1912/13 season proved an outstanding one for the Scot as he became the first Wednesday player to score 30 league goals in a single campaign.

MONDAY 16TH JANUARY 1967

Hartlepool United boss Brian Clough was grateful to Wednesday when they stepped in at the last minute to provide the opposition for a game to officially switch on United's floodlights. The teams drew 3-3 with an own goal from Wilf Smith, in the last minute, ensuring the scores were tied.

SATURDAY 16TH JANUARY 1999

The Owls recorded their best Premiership away win when they beat West Ham 4-0. The home fans were stunned as Andy Hinchcliffe, Petter Rudi, Ritchie Humphreys and a Benito Carbone penalty sealed a superb win.

SATURDAY 17TH JANUARY 1891

Wednesday recorded the biggest win in their history as Lancashire club Halliwell were beaten 12-0 at Olive Grove in the FA Cup. Henry 'Toddles' Woolhouse netted five for Wednesday with Tom and Harry Brandon, Tom Cawley and Albert Mumford amongst the other goalscorers.

WEDNESDAY 17TH JANUARY 1979

The FA Cup marathon with Arsenal continued at Filbert Street as the sides drew 3-3, after extra time, in the fourth instalment of the third round tie.

TUESDAY 17TH JANUARY 1984

Just short of 50,000 fans packed Hillsborough to see league champions Liverpool in an eagerly awaited League Cup quarter-final. They travelled back across the Pennines with a 2-2 draw but only after Wednesday had pushed them all the way with Gary Megson and Gary Bannister scoring.

SATURDAY 18TH JANUARY 1890

Wednesday kicked-off the run to their first FA Cup final with a 6-1 win at Olive Grove against London Swifts. Albert Mumford and Mickey Bennett scored twice.

TUESDAY 18TH JANUARY 1983

The Owls' first appearance in the quarter-finals of the League Cup ended at Highbury as a Tony Woodcock goal, after 68 minutes, sent Arsenal into the last four.

TUESDAY 18TH JANUARY 2000

Many Wednesday fans did not reach Molineux before half-time as horrendous problems on the road – including the closure of the M1 – caused the FA Cup tie against Wolves to be delayed. Luckily, for the majority of the travelling support the game was 0-0 at the break and that was the score after extra time with Wednesday winning 4-3 on penalties. Simon Donnelly scored the decisive kick.

SATURDAY 19TH JANUARY 1878

Wednesday lost 5-1 to Heeley in a friendly played at Sheaf House, while in the Sheffield district of Kiveton Park, Henry 'Harry' Chapman was born into a real football family; his brother, Herbert, became one of the greatest managers of all time with spells at Huddersfield Town and then Arsenal.

MONDAY 19TH JANUARY 1920

Despite Wednesday being bottom in the First Division, a crowd of 52,388 attended the FA Cup replay against non-league Darlington. Unfortunately, they were not rewarded as the minnows won 2-0 in blizzard conditions.

SATURDAY 19TH JANUARY 2002

In a dramatic finale to a First Division game at Burnley, Wednesday had goalkeeper Kevin Pressman carried off after 87 minutes. Rookie keeper Sean Roberts replaced him, Shefki Kuqi scored to put the Owls 2-1 in front, and then Gerald Sibon missed a penalty!

THURSDAY 20TH JANUARY 1910

For the third season running the Owls were knocked out of the FA Cup by lower ranked opposition. Southern League champions Northampton Town delivered the mortal blow on this occasion – a second half goal from Walker being enough to dash hopes in a first round replay.

SATURDAY 20TH JANUARY 1973

The home game with Bristol City was abandoned after 54 minutes due to heavy snow. Just 11,185 fans braved the arctic conditions but did not see any goals before the referee called a halt to proceedings.

WEDNESDAY 20TH JANUARY 1988

A mistake from Owls goalie Martin Hodge gifted Nigel Winterburn the winning goal in the League Cup quarter-final meeting with Arsenal at Hillsborough.

SATURDAY 21ST JANUARY 1893

In a thrilling FA Cup tie at Olive Grove a goal from Fred Spiksley in the last minute of extra time secured a 3-2 win for Wednesday. However, after the game County protested that Owls players Chalmers and Brady were ineligible – the FA ordered the match be replayed, but on neutral territory at Derby.

SATURDAY 21st JANUARY 1899

Derby County's legendary attacker Steve Bloomer hit six goals at the Baseball Ground as Wednesday were beaten 9-0 in a First Division fixture. The defeat is the club's second heaviest in the league.

SATURDAY 21st JANUARY 1961

Incredibly, the Owls took the lead after just 30 seconds at Craven Cottage without even touching the ball! Fulham defender Alan Mullery managed to put through his own goal in record quick time and it was only the start of a disastrous day for the London side as Wednesday won 6-1. Tom McAnearney, John Fantham, Keith Ellis (2) and Alan Finney added to the score.

SATURDAY 22nd JANUARY 1927

The day after signing for Wednesday, Mark Hooper made his debut as a replacement for Rees Williams. The new number seven impressed the Hillsborough faithful as Wednesday shared four goals with visitors Leicester City.

SATURDAY 22nd JANUARY 1955

Struggling Wednesday travelled to White Hart Lane but team plans were in tatters when key wing-half Eddie Gannon could not make the game from his Irish home after his plane was cancelled! Debut forward Don Watson scored for Wednesday but Spurs won 7-2.

SATURDAY 22nd JANUARY 1966

Wednesday needed a last-minute headed goal from John Fantham to clinch a 3-2 FA Cup third round win at Reading.

MONDAY 22nd JANUARY 1979

The third longest tie in the history of the FA Cup finally ended at Filbert Street as eventual winners Arsenal scored twice in the first half to send the gallant Owls side out of the competition in game number five.

SATURDAY 22nd JANUARY 1994

Centre-half Andy Pearce became an unlikely cult hero amongst Owls fans, heading the second goal as Wednesday beat neighbours United 3-1 at Hillsborough in a Premiership contest.

TUESDAY 22ND JANUARY 2002

The Owls' run in the League Cup came to an end at the semi-final stage as Blackburn Rovers won 4-2 at Ewood Park, to reach the final 6-3 on aggregate. Loan keeper Paul Heald made his debut for Wednesday, who netted through Trond Soltvedt and an Efan Ekoku penalty.

SATURDAY 23RD JANUARY 1892

Fred Spiksley's 'official' debut came in the FA Cup game with Bolton Wanderers at Olive Grove. Wednesday won 4-1, with Spiksley scoring twice, and Fred would appear in 321 games for Wednesday with a goal tally of 115, bettered by only six men in the club's history.

SATURDAY 23RD JANUARY 1932

A crowd of 32,600 watched Wednesday beat Bournemouth & Boscombe 7-0 at Hillsborough in the FA Cup with Harry Millership grabbing four goals and Harry Burgess three.

WEDNESDAY 23RD JANUARY 1991

The Owls reached the semi-finals of the League Cup for the first time as a goal from captain Nigel Pearson secured a 1-0 win at First Division Coventry City.

MONDAY 24TH JANUARY 1927

Jackie Sewell was born in Kell, near Whitehaven. He won six England caps during his time at Hillsborough, playing in both seminal games against the magnificent Hungarian side that won 6-3 at Wembley and 7-1 in Budapest.

SATURDAY 24TH JANUARY 1931

Despite a goal from Jack Ball, the Owls lost 2-1 at neighbours Barnsley in an FA Cup fourth round tie. The game marked the final appearance of centre-forward Jack Allen.

SATURDAY 24TH JANUARY 1970

Minnows Scunthorpe United grabbed the headlines as they won 2-1 at top flight Wednesday in the FA Cup fourth round. Led by Kevin Keegan, they came from behind to reach the last sixteen and overshadow what proved to be Don Megson's final appearance for the Owls.

TUESDAY 25th JANUARY 1870

Publican Edward Spiksley no doubt raised a glass to his new son, Fred, born on this day in Gainsborough.

SATURDAY 25th JANUARY 1986

A goal after just 59 seconds by Garry Thompson sent Wednesday on the way to a 5-0 FA Cup win over Orient at Hillsborough.

THURSDAY 26th JANUARY 1956

Although a top-six side in Argentina, San Lorenzo lost 9-0 in a Hillsborough friendly with Alan Finney and Roy Shiner scoring hat-tricks.

MONDAY 26th JANUARY 1987

In a frenetic FA Cup tie at Hillsborough, referee George Courtney incurred the wrath of home fans after controversially sending off Lee Chapman after 44 minutes. The Owls were leading 1-0 at the time and the ten men held on to win.

SATURDAY 26th JANUARY 1991

In a season of memorable games, the Owls drew 4-4 at fellow Second Division side Millwall in an FA Cup fourth round game – Alex Rae equalising for the London club in the final minute.

SATURDAY 27th JANUARY 1923

Ernest Blenkinsop played his first game for Wednesday but it was an unhappy day as Bury won 4-0 at Gigg Lane in a Second Division game.

WEDNESDAY 27th JANUARY 1988

The absence of Lawrie Madden proved decisive as Wednesday crashed out of the FA Cup in the fourth instalment of the third round marathon with Everton. A hat-trick from Graeme Sharp helped the Toffeemen to establish an unassailable 5-0 lead at half-time, at which point many in the 38,953 crowd headed for the local pubs!

SATURDAY 28th JANUARY 1911

Wednesday lost 2-0 at Notts County, in Harry Chapman's last appearance for the club. The outstanding Chapman scored exactly 100 goals in 299 competitive games in a Wednesday shirt.

SATURDAY 28th JANUARY 1967

The 3-0 FA Cup win over Queens Park Rangers saw both Springett brothers between the sticks; Peter in the Owls net and Ron in the Rangers goal.

SATURDAY 29th JANUARY 1983

The Owls won 3-2 in the FA Cup at Fourth Division Torquay United, captain Mick Lyons having put Wednesday ahead after just 39 seconds.

WEDNESDAY 29th JANUARY 1992

Wednesday fans flocked to the Sheffield Arena to glimpse 'bad boy' Eric Cantona, who had joined the Owls on trial. American opponents Baltimore Blast won the six-a-side game 8-3 in front of 8,206 fans.

MONDAY 30th JANUARY 1888

Nine thousand fans watched the 3-1 FA Cup defeat to Preston. It was the first FA Cup game to be played at Olive Grove; Billy Ingram netted the first competitive goal at Wednesday's new home.

WEDNESDAY 30th JANUARY 1946

Wednesday won 6-1 at York City in the FA Cup fourth round. A Charlie Tomlinson treble helped the Owls to an 11-2 aggregate win in the only season when the tournament was played over two legs in the early stages.

WEDNESDAY 30th JANUARY 1985

In a momentous League Cup tie at Hillsborough, Wednesday and Chelsea shared eight goals. The Owls led 3-0 at the interval and looked on course for their first-ever semi-final appearance but the Pensioners hit back to lead 4-3 before a last-minute penalty from Mel Sterland meant extra time.

SATURDAY 31st JANUARY 1903

Two goals from Harry Chapman and one from Harry Davis secured a 3-1 top-flight win over Liverpool at Hillsborough. Meanwhile, outstanding centre-forward John William Alcroft Allen was born in Newcastle.

WEDNESDAY 31st JANUARY 1934

A Hillsborough crowd of 41,311 saw the Owls comprehensively beat Oldham Athletic 6-1 in the FA Cup.

SHEFFIELD WEDNESDAY
On This Day

FEBRUARY

SATURDAY 1st FEBRUARY 1896

At the Antelope Grounds, Wednesday won 3-2 against non-league Southampton St. Mary's with Alec Brady (2) and Harry Davis netting.

SATURDAY 1st FEBRUARY 1958

Wednesday, bottom of the First Division, gave a debut to teenager John Fantham for the home game with Tottenham Hotspur. He enjoyed a winning start as goals from Derek Wilkinson and Roy Shiner secured a much-needed 2-0 win.

WEDNESDAY 1st FEBRUARY 1961

After a 1-1 draw at Hillsborough on the previous Saturday, the Owls travelled to Manchester United to replay an FA Cup tie. The crowd of 65,243 were left stunned as Wednesday recorded a 7-2 win thanks to goals from Keith Ellis (3), John Fantham (2) and Alan Finney (2).

THURSDAY 2nd FEBRUARY 1893

The third instalment of the FA Cup tie with Derby County was played at Olive Grove after the FA ordered another match following the Owls' successful appeal, after they had lost at County 48 hours earlier. This time Wednesday did reach the next round, winning 4-2.

SATURDAY 2nd FEBRUARY 1907

In a tricky FA Cup tie at non-league Southampton St. Mary's, Wednesday needed a last-minute equaliser from Andrew Wilson, in front of 15,000 at the Dell, to force a replay.

SATURDAY 2nd FEBRUARY 1929

Centre-forward Jimmy Trotter played his last match for Wednesday in front of 44,576 at Bramall Lane, as the city clubs drew 1-1. The point kept Wednesday on top of the First Division table while for Trotter it was his 159th and last game. He scored an outstanding 114 goals.

MONDAY 2nd FEBRUARY 1976

With Wednesday struggling in the Third Division, they could have done with the services of pre-war hero Jack Ball who died in Luton on this day. His record of ten successful penalty kicks in the 1932/33 season stood for almost fifty years.

THURSDAY 3RD FEBRUARY 1921

A new record crowd for the city of Sheffield was set when 62,407 fans packed into Hillsborough for the FA Cup replay with Everton. The Toffeemen, however, progressed through to the next round, winning 1-0.

SATURDAY 3RD FEBRUARY 1923

Exactly two years after setting the previous best crowd figure, it was smashed as 66,103 flooded into Hillsborough for an eagerly awaited FA Cup clash with neighbours Barnsley. The Tykes led at the break but second-half strikes from Andy Smailes and Sid Binks secured passage for the Owls with the final whistle triggering a joyous pitch invasion.

SATURDAY 4TH FEBRUARY 1939

For only the third time since 1919, two players of the same side were sent off as Bradford Park Avenue men George Stabb and Bill Hallard were ordered off within a minute of each other, just after the interval. Wednesday took advantage of the numerical difference to score twice and win 2-0, moving up to fourth place in the Second Division table.

WEDNESDAY 4TH FEBRUARY 1987

The 3-1 FA Cup replay win over Third Division Chester City was marred by a horrific injury to Wednesday defender Ian Knight. A reckless tackle from Gary Bennett left Knight with multiple leg fractures – injuries more akin to a road traffic accident – which left Knight with his right leg one inch shorter than his left and his highly promising career in tatters.

SATURDAY 4TH FEBRUARY 2006

In almost comical circumstances, the Owls won 1-0 at Millwall in a crucial relegation battle at the foot of the Championship. As Millwall players celebrated what seemed like a goal in the 62nd minute, the Owls took a quick free kick (the referee had disallowed the goal) and with the Lions totally disorganised, broke upfield to take the lead through a scrambled effort from Frank Simek. The Owls already had Lee Bullen in goal after David Lucas was carried off in the early stages, but held on for a tremendous win.

WEDNESDAY 5TH FEBRUARY 1913

The Owls welcomed Chelsea to Hillsborough for their replayed FA Cup second round game, the teams having tied 1-1 in London four days earlier. There was no mercy from Wednesday on this occasion as the Pensioners were beaten 6-0 with the local press stating; "so one-sided was the game that the great crowd was never roused to excitement."The crowd numbered 35,860 with top scorer David McLean grabbing his second treble of that season's FA Cup campaign.

SATURDAY 5TH FEBRUARY 2000

Owls fans were left stunned at Pride Park as relegation rivals Derby County somehow scored twice in added time to rescue a 3-3 draw.Wednesday had looked certain to gain a vital win and for many fans the late capitulation would prove a mortal blow to the club's battle to avoid relegation.

MONDAY 6TH FEBRUARY 1939

Sheffield Wednesday's post-war top scorer, John Fantham, was born in Sheffield. He would spend over thirteen years with Wednesday, scoring 166 goals in 434 appearances.

SATURDAY 6TH FEBRUARY 1960

Norman Curtis, after 21 goals in 324 games, played his last game for Wednesday in a 2-2 home draw with Everton. His pass set up Tony Kay for the opening goal while a Tom McAnearney penalty ensured honours were shared.

TUESDAY 6TH FEBRUARY 1979

After the energy sapping FA Cup marathon with Arsenal, manager Jack Charlton took his troops for a mini break in Guernsey, the Owls beating local side Vale Recreation 5-0 in a friendly encounter.

SATURDAY 6TH FEBRUARY 1982

The game of the 1981/82 season was played at Hillsborough as promotion chasing Wednesday drew 3-3 with league leaders Luton Town.The Owls were twice behind before a Gary Bannister strike after 83 minutes looked set to steal the points. However, two minutes into added time Mark Stein fired home to grab a point for the eventual champions.

TUESDAY 7TH FEBRUARY 1882

Wednesday beat Upton Park 6-0 at Bramall Lane to reach their first FA Cup semi-final. A hat-trick from Tom Cawley, Billy Mosforth (2) and a Rhodes goal completed the scoring. In the previous month Rhodes had become the first Wednesday player to score more than three goals in a competitive fixture when he netted four in a 5-1 win at Staveley.

SATURDAY 7TH FEBRUARY 2004

It was a bad day at the office for Wednesday as David Lucas was carried off with a serious knee injury, Adam Proudlock was red carded after 48 minutes, and hosts Port Vale registered a 3-0 win.

SATURDAY 7TH FEBRUARY 2009

The wait for a league double over rivals Sheffield United was finally at an end after 95 years. A first-minute goal from boyhood Wednesday fan Tommy Spurr and a wonder strike from top scorer Marcus Tudgay sealed a 2-1 win at Bramall Lane in front of 30,786, plus 9,000 Wednesday fans at the Hillsborough beam back.

SATURDAY 8TH FEBRUARY 1933

The Owls beat Leeds United 2-0 at Hillsborough. Both goals were penalties converted by centre-forward Jack Ball who set a club record of ten successful spot kicks – he also missed four times during the 1932/33 campaign.

WEDNESDAY 8TH FEBRUARY 1995

Despite leading 3-0 in a penalty shoot out at Wolves, Wednesday incredibly managed to lose 4-3 after the FA Cup replay had ended 1-1. Andy Pearce, Chris Bart-Williams and Chris Waddle were the guilty parties as the home side gained an unlikely passage.

SATURDAY 9TH FEBRUARY 1907

Wednesday crashed 8-1 at Aston Villa in a First Division game. Winger Harry Davis had actually equalised for the Owls after 10 minutes but the home side romped away with Harry Hampton bagging a treble in front of 20,000 at Villa Park.

SATURDAY 9TH FEBRUARY 1952

Wednesday recovered from a two goal deficit to beat Cardiff City 4-2 at Hillsborough. Inside-forward Jackie Sewell scored all four as the Owls moved into first position in the Second Division table.

SATURDAY 10TH FEBRUARY 1900

The all Sheffield FA Cup derby at Bramall Lane fell victim to the weather as heavy snow resulted in the tie being abandoned after 53 minutes, with neither side having scored. A bumper crowd of almost 33,000 were inside the ground for the eagerly awaited clash but despite the teams going off the field for 15 minutes the conditions failed to improve and the referee called a halt to proceedings.

SATURDAY 10TH FEBRUARY 1934

Sporting white shirts with blue collars Wednesday held Newcastle United to a 0-0 score at St. James' Park. The draw meant the Owls had equalled their 1899 record of 16 games unbeaten.

SUNDAY 10TH FEBRUARY 1974

The visit of Bristol City to Hillsborough proved a historic occasion as Wednesday played their first ever league fixture on the Sabbath. A higher than average crowd of 15,888 watched the proceedings with Brian Joicey, Willie Henderson and Bernard Shaw scoring in a 3-1 victory.

WEDNESDAY 10TH FEBRUARY 1993

In a devastating spell of attacking football the Owls scored four times in just 16 minutes to effectively settle their League Cup semi-final first leg tie at Blackburn Rovers. The Ewood Park side netted either side of the salvo as Wednesday won 4-2 to put one foot in the final.

SATURDAY 10TH FEBRUARY 2001

Wednesday went two goals behind inside the first nine minutes of the away game at Wimbledon as loan goalie Marlon Beresford scored a second-half own goal as the Owls lost 4-1 at Selhurst Park. The result left Wednesday 24th in Division One and marked the end of Paul Jewell's short tenure in the managerial hot seat.

TUESDAY 10TH FEBRUARY 2004

A late goal from Blackpool's Scott Taylor gave the home side a 1-0 advantage to take to Hillsborough, after the first leg of the Associate Members Cup Northern Final at Bloomfield Road.

SATURDAY 11TH FEBRUARY 1950

Club trainer Bill Knox died suddenly of a heart attack at his Sheffield home. He had joined the Owls in 1947, from Huddersfield Town, and helped generate the revival that saw the club promoted in 1950. Sadly he did not live to see the fruits of his labour, passing away aged just 44.

SATURDAY 11TH FEBRUARY 1984

In front of the *Match of the Day* cameras, the Owls continued their great form at the top of the Second Division – beating visitors Charlton Athletic 4-1 with Imre Varadi scoring one of the goals of the season executing an inch perfect lob over the visiting goalkeeper. Strikes from Gary Bannister, Peter Shirtliff and Tony Cunningham had already put Wednesday three goals ahead before Varadi provided the icing on the cake.

TUESDAY 12TH FEBRUARY 1935

On a somewhat bizarre afternoon at Hillsborough the Owls held a public practice game with the whites beating the stripes 4-1. The club had arranged the match after being drawn at Norwich City in the fifth round of the FA Cup and manager Billy Walker wanted to simulate the tight, cramped surrounding of the Norfolk club's Nest ground. To replicate this, the pitch size was reduced and spectators were encouraged to stand close to the pitch, encroaching by up to ten yards during the two-hour game. As all this unfolded, Walker sat in the scoreboard, at the Leppings Lane end, barking out instructions through a microphone!

SATURDAY 12TH FEBRUARY 1949

As the post-war boom in attendances continued, a crowd of 49,980 were at Hillsborough to see a Sheffield County Cup semi-final against Sheffield United. The Blades raced into a 4-0 half-time lead and despite Eddie Quigley netting twice for Wednesday their top flight rivals prevailed.

SATURDAY 12TH FEBRUARY 1966

A week after losing at St. James' Park in the league, Wednesday returned to the north-east to record a surprise 2-0 win in the FA Cup fourth round. Watched by a 39,500 crowd, a goal from Colin Dobson and a John McGrath own goal sent the Owls into the last sixteen.

MONDAY 12TH FEBRUARY 2001

After less than a season in charge, manager Paul Jewell was sacked from his post after only 31 league games.

MONDAY 13TH FEBRUARY 1922

New signing Jimmy Trotter made his Wednesday debut in the home game with Wolves. Trotter scored two minutes after half-time and the Owls won 3-1 with a Tom Brelsford penalty and a great individual goal from Charlie Petrie.

SATURDAY 13TH FEBRUARY 1943

In a wartime game at Hillsborough, the Owls beat Sheffield United 8-2 with Jackie Robinson notching a hat-trick. A healthy crowd of 18,232 witnessed the club's biggest win over their rivals in a senior game.

SUNDAY 13TH FEBRUARY 1994

A first-half strike from Ryan Giggs proved the only goal of the first leg of the League Cup semi-final between Wednesday and Manchester United at Old Trafford.

SATURDAY 14TH FEBRUARY 1903

With Harry Davis away on international duty, Wednesday promoted Jimmy Stewart from the reserves, for his debut, against Grimsby Town at Owlerton. A first-half penalty from Ambrose Langley put the home side ahead but the Mariners hit back to equalise with just four minutes left. The point left the Owls second in the top flight.

SATURDAY 14TH FEBRUARY 1953

In the First Division game at Deepdale, the Owls lost to a Tom Finney goal after 80 minutes but the day was defined in the 59th minute when star centre-forward Derek Dooley broke his right leg after a collision with Preston goalkeeper George Thompson, and was taken to Preston Royal Infirmary.

SATURDAY 14TH FEBRUARY 1998

Eighteen-year-old Michael Owen stole the show at Hillsborough as he grabbed a hat-tick in a thrilling 3-3 Premiership draw against Liverpool.

SATURDAY 14TH FEBRUARY 2004

An Owls fan decided to surprise his girlfriend on Valentine's Day by proposing to her at half-time of the 1-0 League One win against Hartlepool United. She said "yes" but the Kop sang; "You don't know what you're doing!"

SATURDAY 15TH FEBRUARY 1868

Wednesday appeared in the Bramall Lane final of the four-team Cromwell Cup. The competition's benefactor, Oliver Cromwell, was a member of the Carrick Club and it was his side that faced Wednesday in front of 600 fans. With the score tied 0-0 at full time the sides agreed to play on until a winning goal was scored and it was Wednesday who grabbed the winner – therefore scoring a 'golden goal' some 129 years before FIFA introduced the rule!

SATURDAY 15TH FEBRUARY 1896

Wednesday took another step on their way to the cup final by beating Sunderland 2-1 at Olive Grove. Goals from Lawrie Bell and Fred Spiksley secured the win in front of 22,000 fans.

SATURDAY 15TH FEBRUARY 1992

In an almost surreal game at Highbury, the Owls and Arsenal were drawing 1-1 with just 19 minutes left to play in a First Division encounter. However, in that short time the Londoners somehow managed to crash home six goals to leave a shell shocked away support to trek back up the M1 after a 7-1 defeat!

SATURDAY 16TH FEBRUARY 1895

Both Sheffield teams played at home in the FA Cup with Wednesday kicking off their tie against Middlesbrough at 2.30 pm and United starting an hour later. The early start suited Wednesday as they convincingly won 6-1 to reach the last eight of the competition. Harry Davis scored three with match receipts totalling £107, 8 shillings and threepence.

SATURDAY 16TH FEBRUARY 1901

New centre-forward Harry Chapman scored on his debut as Blackburn Rovers held Wednesday to a 1-1 scoreline at Hillsborough. An estimated crowd of 7,000 watched the game with an unfortunate own goal after 87 minutes denying the home side both points.

THURSDAY 16TH FEBRUARY 1911

Wednesday broke the £1,000 transfer barrier for the first time signing centre-forward David McLean from Preston North End.

SATURDAY 16TH FEBRUARY 1935

The FA Cup meeting between Norwich City and Wednesday generated a record crowd and record receipts (25,007 and £2,387 respectively) for City's old ground of 'The Nest'. The Second Division Canaries could not produce a cup shock though as a 74th minute goal from Ellis Rimmer sent Wednesday through to the last eight.

SATURDAY 16TH FEBRUARY 1952

Almost 30,000 packed into Oakwell to watch the local derby against Second Division leaders Wednesday. In an action-packed game Barnsley led twice before Matthew McNeil headed home an 88th-minute winner to win the points for The Tykes after a nine-goal thriller.

SATURDAY 17TH FEBRUARY 1900

After the first game was abandoned Wednesday and Sheffield United suffered two more postponements before the sides drew 1-1 at Bramall Lane in their second round FA Cup tie.

SATURDAY 17TH FEBRUARY 1934

Hillsborough was packed to the rafters for the FA Cup fifth round meeting with Manchester City. The crowd figure reached 72,841 to set a ground record that will never be beaten. The cup tie was a thriller as the teams shared four goals with Ellis Rimmer and Neil Dewar netting for Wednesday. Over 68,000 saw the replay four days later that City won 2-0 on their way to winning the trophy. The game also saw the Owls set a new record of 17 games unbeaten.

TUESDAY 17th FEBRUARY 1953

The football world was stunned when doctors at Preston Royal Infirmary had no choice but to amputate the right leg of Wednesday hero Derek Dooley, to save his life. He remained critically ill for several days but recovered to re-build his shattered life.

SATURDAY 17th FEBRUARY 1990

Arsenal defender Steve Bould scored the quickest own goal seen at Hillsborough as he deflected Nigel Worthington's header into his own net after just 15 seconds! The early faux pas proved the only goal of the game as Wednesday won 1-0.

MONDAY 18th FEBRUARY 1878

Wednesday welcomed Glasgow Rangers to Bramall Lane for a cross border challenge match. The Scots won 2-1 with Patterson netting for The Wednesday.

SATURDAY 18th FEBRUARY 1911

A first-half goal from Owls defender Jimmy Spoors secured a 1-0 First Division home win over Bury as the club gave debuts to two new players; centre-forward David McLean and half-back Jimmy Campbell.

SATURDAY 18th FEBRUARY 1967

At the age of 16 years, 257 days, rookie goalkeeper Gary Scothorn became the youngest player to appear in a first team game for Wednesday. He kept a clean sheet as the Stags were beaten 4-0, in front of over 49,000 fans.

SATURDAY 18th FEBRUARY 1989

The Owls' woes from the penalty spot continued as Southampton keeper John Burridge saved Mel Sterland's effort – Wednesday failed to find the net from any of the four penalties awarded during the 1988/89 campaign.

MONDAY 19th FEBRUARY 1900

In arguably the fiercest derby game ever played in Sheffield, Wednesday and United locked horns at Hillsborough in a replayed FA Cup tie. The Owls had both Jack Pryce and Ambrose Langley sent off as United won 2-0 while Wednesday ended the game with just eight men as George Lee suffered a first-half broken leg.

WEDNESDAY 19TH FEBRUARY 1958

On an emotional evening at Old Trafford, the Owls provided the first opposition for Manchester United since the Munich air disaster. An understandably makeshift United side won 3-0 in the FA Cup fifth round tie. The match programme showed the poignancy of the evening by leaving the United team blank.

MONDAY 19TH FEBRUARY 1973

With Wednesday fans dominating the Villa Park crowd of 19,151, the Owls knocked top flight Crystal Palace out of the FA Cup in the fourth round, second replay. A hat-trick from Brian Joicey sent Wednesday through with the winner hitting the net after 109 minutes.

SATURDAY 20TH FEBRUARY 1904

In the FA Cup, Wednesday crashed six goals past Manchester United without reply. An Owlerton crowd of 22,051 saw Wednesday amateur player Vivian Simpson score a hat-trick – sadly he was lost in the Great War, being killed in France in April 1918.

SATURDAY 20TH FEBRUARY 1909

With a place in the last eight of the FA Cup at stake, the Owls lost 1-0 at home to Second Division Glossop North End, in front of a 35,019 crowd. The Owls missed two penalties (Tom Brittleton and Harry Burton) and the new 'lucky mascot' – a live monkey dressed in blue and white – made his first and last appearance!

SATURDAY 20TH FEBRUARY 1965

In a poor game at Hillsborough, visitors Everton won 1-0. The match also marked the end of Tom McAnearney's Wednesday career although he would return to Hillsborough later in the decade to become assistant manager, and then caretaker boss.

THURSDAY 21ST FEBRUARY 1963

With Britain in the grip of one of the worst winters on record, the Owls played only once in February, drawing 1-1 at Shrewsbury Town in a much delayed FA Cup third round tie. A header from Bronco Layne earned the Owls a draw against their Division Three opponents.

SATURDAY 21st FEBRUARY 1998

Wednesday beat Tottenham Hotspur 1-0 at Hillsborough in the Premiership. Just under 30,000 fans watched the action as Paolo Di Canio's 33rd-minute strike meant all three points stayed in Sheffield.

TUESDAY 22nd FEBRUARY 1955

One of the club's greatest players, Tom Brittleton, died in Winsford, Cheshire.

SATURDAY 22nd FEBRUARY 1997

Wednesday recovered from two goals down to win a game for the first time since 1963, as Southampton were beaten 3-2 at the Dell. The Saints led 2-0 at the interval but the Owls stormed back to take the three points thanks to a David Hirst brace and an Andy Booth close range strike.

SATURDAY 23rd FEBRUARY 1907

In front of a bumper cup crowd of 36,324 the Owls drew 0-0 with fellow top flight side Sunderland in an FA Cup third round tie at Hillsborough.

WEDNESDAY 23rd FEBRUARY 1972

Sick notes, doctor's appointments and dentist visits must have abounded in Sheffield on this day as Pele and his Santos team rolled into town for an afternoon friendly game. Almost 37,000 attended the match, which the Brazilians won 2-0 in a rather low-key encounter.

SATURDAY 24th FEBRUARY 1894

Cup fever gripped Sheffield as 22,100 fans filled Olive Grove to see cup holders Aston Villa face Wednesday in a quarter-final tie. The huge crowd were rewarded as Fred Spiksley equalised with just two minutes remaining, forcing the match into an extra thirty minutes with the score tied at 2-2. With five minutes left Olive Grove erupted as Harry Woolhouse sent Wednesday into their fourth semi-final.

SATURDAY 24th FEBRUARY 1951

A crowd of just under 41,000 watched the Owls share four goals with Chelsea at Hillsborough in a top flight fixture. The game saw both Alan Finney and Albert Quixall make their first team debuts with the latter scoring after 60 minutes to put Wednesday 2-1 ahead.

SUNDAY 24TH FEBRUARY 1991

Wednesday fans were up early for a noon kick-off in the League Cup semi-final first leg at Chelsea. The early start was rewarded, however, with a 2-0 win, goals from Peter Shirtliff and David Hirst making the Owls favourites for Wembley.

SATURDAY 25TH FEBRUARY 1928

Mark Hooper and Ellis Rimmer played their first game together as the latter made his debut in the First Division meeting with Newcastle United. A poor game ended 0-0 to leave the Owls still bottom of the league and facing almost certain relegation.

SATURDAY 25TH FEBRUARY 1984

New signing Nigel Worthington made his debut in the 2-1 win over Brighton & Hove Albion at Hillsborough. He had joined for £100,000 from Notts County earlier in the month.

SATURDAY 25TH FEBRUARY 1989

It was a day of milestones at Wimbledon. Before the lowest top flight crowd of the season – 4,384 – the Owls gave a debut to new signing Carlton Palmer and said goodbye to Mel Sterland, as the Dons won 1-0.

WEDNESDAY 25TH FEBRUARY 2004

A bumper crowd, for the competition, of 21,390 were at Hillsborough for the second leg of the Northern Final of the Associate Members Cup. Unfortunately, Blackpool scored twice in the first period to end any hopes of a trip to Cardiff.

SATURDAY 26TH FEBRUARY 1972

A hat-trick from Wednesday left winger John Sissons was not enough to earn any points at Turf Moor as Burnley won 5-3 in a Second Division game.

SATURDAY 26TH FEBRUARY 1983

Owls centre-forward Andy McCulloch missed a glorious chance of recording a hat-trick as he missed a last-minute penalty, as Cambridge United were beaten 3-1 at Hillsborough in a Second Division game.

WEDNESDAY 26TH FEBRUARY 1986

In a controversial FA Cup tie – played on a rock hard, icy surface – Wednesday drew 1-1 at Derby County. A second-half head injury to Owls keeper Martin Hodge saw the game held up for five minutes but the brave goalie battled on to help take the Third Division opponents to a replay.

WEDNESDAY 27TH FEBRUARY 1907

A goal from left-winger George Simpson gave Wednesday a 1-0 win on Wearside as Sunderland were beaten to send the Owls into the last eight of the FA Cup.

WEDNESDAY 27TH FEBRUARY 1991

On one of the greatest nights in Wednesday's history, the Owls were roared to a 3-1 win over Chelsea in the second leg of the League Cup semi-final. The result clinched a 5-1 aggregate success and sent the large majority of the 34,669 crowd home in very high spirits.

WEDNESDAY 28TH FEBRUARY 1962

Poor weather meant only 28,956 were inside Hillsborough for the visit of Spanish giants Barcelona in the Fairs Cup quarter-finals. A brace from John Fantham and one from Alan Finney took Wednesday to a 3-2 win to leave the tie finely balanced.

SATURDAY 28TH FEBRUARY 2009

Wednesday won 4-2 at promotion chasing Burnley in a Championship encounter. Man of the Match, Leon Clarke, scored twice while Marcus Tudgay also grabbed a brace to delight the travelling 1,843 Owls.

SATURDAY 29TH FEBRUARY 1896

Wednesday comprehensively progressed to the last four of the FA Cup after Everton were beaten 4-0 at Olive Grove. Two goals apiece from Lawrie Bell and Archie Brash did the damage for the home side.

SATURDAY 29TH FEBRUARY 1992

In front of just 17,538 at Stamford Bridge, the Owls outplayed Chelsea to record a 3-0 win with the three Ws – Worthington, Williams and Wilson – all finding the net to keep Wednesday in the hunt for the title.

SHEFFIELD WEDNESDAY
On This Day

MARCH

MONDAY 1st MARCH 1915

In a First Division game with Bolton Wanderers at Hillsborough, the Owls recorded a comprehensive 7-0 win with seven different men finding the net. David Parkes, Teddy Glennon, Jimmy Gill, George Robertson, Andrew Wilson, Alf Capper and Harry Bentley all scored on a unique afternoon.

SATURDAY 1st MARCH 1952

It was another goal-laden afternoon for Derek Dooley as he scored four times to help beat Hull City 6-0 at Hillsborough. A brace from Jackie Sewell completed the scoring in front of 41,811 fans.

TUESDAY 1st MARCH 1983

Wednesday lost 1-0 at Wolves in a game of three penalties and a controversial sending off. Wolves successfully converted from the spot but Gary Bannister saw both of his penalties saved by John Burridge – including one in the final minute – while captain Mick Lyons was sent from the field for the only time in his long career.

SATURDAY 2nd MARCH 1878

Wednesday retained the Sheffield Challenge Cup when goals from Butler and Bishop sealed a 2-0 win against Attercliffe in the final at Bramall Lane.

SATURDAY 2nd MARCH 1935

In a titanic battle at Hillsborough, goals from wingers Mark Hooper and Ellis Rimmer secured a 2-1 win over Arsenal, in front of 66,945 fans, to send Wednesday through to the FA Cup semi-finals.

SATURDAY 2nd MARCH 1957

Despite Wednesday losing 3-1 at Blackpool it was a day to remember for debutant Gerry Young. In sixteen years he racked up 344 games, scoring 20 times, before being co-opted onto the coaching staff in 1971. He was briefly caretaker manager in December 1973 but was dismissed in October 1975 along with manager Steve Burtenshaw.

WEDNESDAY 2nd MARCH 1994

Hopes of reaching Wembley ended in the second leg of the League Cup semi-final as visitors Manchester United scored twice in the first 11 minutes and went on to win 4-1, and 5-1 on aggregate.

SATURDAY 3RD MARCH 1934

It was a disastrous day for Wednesday as they were beaten 5-1 at Bramall Lane in front of 32,318. The Owls led through a Horace Burrows goal until midway through the second half but a Bill Boyd treble led the way as Wednesday's defence collapsed like a deck of cards!

SATURDAY 3RD MARCH 1999

Visitors to Hillsborough, Wimbledon, pre sold only 32 tickets for the Premiership game but the tiny pocket of away fans went home happy as the Dons won 2-1; future Owl Efan Ekoku netted for the visitors. Unfortunately for Wimbledon boss Joe Kinnear he did not see the win, being rushed to hospital pre-match after suffering a heart attack.

SATURDAY 3RD MARCH 2007

An astonishing 35-yard effort from Chris Brunt, from near the touchline, was the highlight of a superb 3-2 win at Leeds United. Wednesday led 2-0 when Marcus Tudgay was inexplicably sent off for time-wasting but Jermaine Johnson scored a superb third although the away side did experience some late jitters, as United scored twice in the last two minutes.

SATURDAY 4TH MARCH 1933

Wednesday player Tony Leach was sent off after an hour's play at Hillsborough as the Owls beat Wolves 2-0 to remain second in the First Division.

SATURDAY 4TH MARCH 1939

In the last league derby meeting before the Second World War, Wednesday beat United 1-0 at Hillsborough – a 78th minute goal from Bill Fallon sealing the points for the Owls.

SATURDAY 4TH MARCH 1972

Tommy Craig sent the Preston North End keeper the wrong way from his 75th minute penalty to earn Wednesday a 1-0 Second Division win in front of 12,162.

SATURDAY 5TH MARCH 1955

In a reserve game at Burnley, a home supporter played for Wednesday after two of their chosen side, undertaking National Service, failed to report for the game!

SATURDAY 5TH MARCH 1966

A huge following from Sheffield were in the Leeds Road crowd of 49,612 as the Owls beat Huddersfield Town 2-1 to reach the quarter-final of the FA Cup. A first minute goal from Stephen Smith had put the Terriers ahead but David Ford levelled after 53 minutes and Brian Usher slid home the winner with ten minutes remaining.

WEDNESDAY 5TH MARCH 1986

Virtual unknown Carl Shutt grabbed the national headlines as his brace gave Wednesday a 2-0 FA Cup fifth round replay win over Derby County at Hillsborough, sealing a quarter-final place.

WEDNESDAY 5TH MARCH 2008

Sheffield football legend Derek Dooley died in Sheffield, aged 78. His 63 goals in 63 games for Wednesday marked Dooley as one of the club's greatest-ever goalscorers while he became revered on the other side of the city during spells on the board of directors and as chairman.

MONDAY 6TH MARCH 1882

In the club's first FA Cup semi-final appearance, Blackburn Rovers were held to a 0-0 draw at the Huddersfield Rugby Ground, in front of 6,000 fans.

WEDNESDAY 6TH MARCH 1996

Dreadlocked winger Regi Blinker made a dream Owls debut, scoring twice – but Wednesday lost 3-2 at Aston Villa in the Premier League.

SATURDAY 7TH MARCH 1908

One of the most popular players in the club's history, Tommy Crawshaw, ended his career at Wednesday on a high as in his farewell appearance, goals from Andrew Wilson and James Maxwell secured a 2-0 derby win over the Blades in front of 20,000 fans at Hillsborough. During 14 years at Wednesday, Crawshaw won 10 England caps and after retiring ran several public houses in Sheffield.

SATURDAY 7TH MARCH 1914

A new record Hillsborough crowd of 56,991 – generating receipts of £2,302 – watched Wednesday lose 1-0 to Aston Villa in an FA Cup quarter-final clash.

SATURDAY 8TH MARCH 1890

In front of 15,000 at Aston Villa's old Perry Barr ground, Wednesday beat Bolton Wanderers 2-1 to reach their first FA Cup final. A 70th minute goal from Cassidy had put the Wanderers ahead but Harry Winterbottom equalised two minutes later and Albert Mumford hit the winner after 80 minutes.

SATURDAY 8TH MARCH 1986

Carl Shutt took his goals tally to five in two games after grabbing his first senior hat-trick as Birmingham City were beaten 5-1 in a First Division game at Hillsborough.

MONDAY 8TH MARCH 1993

The Owls and Derby County drew 3-3 at the Baseball Ground in a thrilling FA Cup sixth round tie. Wednesday were twice ahead but their First Division opponents hit back to take the lead only for Paul Warhurst to force a replay by levelling matters in the 85th minute.

SATURDAY 8TH MARCH 2003

Paul McLaren achieved the relatively rare feat of scoring at both ends in the Owls' 1-1 draw at Leicester City. He had put his side ahead with a long-range drive after 25 minutes but could only watch in horror as his back pass to keeper Paul Evans, from near the centre circle, was totally missed by the goalkeeper and slowly trickled into the net!

SATURDAY 9TH MARCH 1907

A new crowd record was set for Owlerton (37,830) as Liverpool visited for an eagerly awaited FA Cup quarter-final tie. The Owls duly progressed 1-0 with match-winner Harry Chapman carried off the pitch at the end by the delighted home fans.

WEDNESDAY 9TH MARCH 1955

The first game played under floodlights at Hillsborough saw a Sheffield XI face an International XI for the benefit of Derek Dooley. A crowd of 55,000 attended the game with Tommy Lawton and Eddie Quigley amongst the scorers for the International team as they romped to a 5-1 win.

SATURDAY 9th MARCH 1974

Relegation threatened Wednesday stunned their own followers by recording a 5-1 win at Notts County, thanks to two goals apiece for Mick Prendergast and Brian Joicey plus one from Eric Potts. The two points lifted the Owls up one place to 19th in the Second Division. The day also brought forth sad news as inter-war winger Mark Hooper passed away, aged 72. After his playing days ended he opened a sweet and tobacconists shop on Middlewood Road, near Hillsborough, where he served Wednesday fans for almost forty years.

SATURDAY 10th MARCH 1877

The inaugural final of the new Sheffield Challenge Cup competition was held at Bramall Lane and Heeley looked certain to be the first winners after racing into a 3-0 lead at the interval. However, Wednesday came back in sensational style and an extra time goal from Skinner clinched a 4-3 win to ensure The Wednesday would be the first name inscribed on the new £50 trophy.

SATURDAY 10th MARCH 1894

A large contingent of Wednesday fans travelled across the Pennines, swelling the crowd at the Fallowfield Ground to over 30,000, to watch the FA Cup semi-final clash with Bolton Wanderers. Unfortunately, despite a late goal from Harry Woolhouse sparking a late fightback they failed to turn around a two-goal deficit, exiting the competition 2-1.

WEDNESDAY 10th MARCH 1920

Andrew Wilson played as an emergency forward in the 1-0 defeat at Liverpool, his final game in an Owls shirt. Although he had appeared in 75 wartime games for the club his last competitive game was back in April 1915 – 'Andra' having been co-opted onto the coaching staff in 1919.

SUNDAY 11th MARCH 1984

The dour 0-0 FA Cup sixth round draw with Southampton, watched by 43,030 at Hillsborough, was the first game ever to be televised live from the ground.

SATURDAY 11TH MARCH 2000

Paolo Di Canio played at Hillsborough for the first time since pushing referee Paul Alcock. Unfortunately, it was in a West Ham United shirt but it was a rare good day for Wednesday fans in a season of strife – the Owls winning 3-1.

MONDAY 12TH MARCH 1900

Henry Bolsover made his debut for Wednesday, as Burton Swifts were thrashed 6-0 at Owlerton, with six different men finding the net. The Sheffield club keeper made his second and final appearance five days later but achieved great success in 1904 when he was in the Sheffield side that won the FA Amateur Cup.

SATURDAY 12TH MARCH 1938

Conditions were so bad at Upton Park that the referee cut the half-time interval to just seven minutes as heavy rain threatened to cause an abandonment of the West Ham v. Wednesday game. The match did, however, reach a conclusion with the Hammers winning 1-0 in a game that saw Ellis Rimmer make his final appearance for Wednesday.

SATURDAY 12TH MARCH 2005

Nineteen-year-old substitute Drew Talbot stole the show at Hillsborough as he scored twice in the last eight minutes against Blackpool, after replacing James Quinn just past the hour, to clinch a vital 3-2 win in the club's chase for automatic promotion. The game also saw loan full-back Alex Bruce make his debut as did reserve keeper Chris Adamson, who replaced the injured David Lucas after just eight minutes.

MONDAY 13TH MARCH 1899

Wednesday and Aston Villa met at Olive Grove to play the remaining 10½ minutes of their league game. After the first game was abandoned – with Wednesday winning 3-1 – the Football League bizarrely ordered the remaining minutes to be played at a later date. This duly occurred with Fred Richards netting an additional goal to leave Wednesday as 4-1 winners. After the time had been played out the sides met in a benefit match for Wednesday player Harry Davis, the game consisting of two 35-minute periods.

SATURDAY 13TH MARCH 1926

The visit of Second Division leaders Wednesday to Oakwell resulted in Barnsley setting a new record gate for a league fixture (28,124). A first-half Jimmy Trotter goal earned the Owls a point to keep them in pole position.

TUESDAY 13TH MARCH 1945

The club's record goalscorer, Andrew Wilson, died, aged 64, at Patterton Farm, near Irvine. His goals tally of 216 is fifty more than any other Wednesday player.

SATURDAY 14TH MARCH 1987

A 48,005 crowd (including 15,000 visitors) packed into Hillsborough for the FA Cup quarter-final clash between Wednesday and Coventry City. It was, however, to be Coventry's year and a late double from Keith Houchen sealed a 3-1 win for the eventual winners, after Gary Megson had equalised.

SATURDAY 14TH MARCH 1992

Goals from David Hirst – his 100th Wednesday goal – and Paul Williams helped the Owls to a 2-0 win at Spurs, keeping hopes alive of a top-three finish.

WEDNESDAY 15TH MARCH 1882

In the FA Cup semi-final replay against Blackburn Rovers – held at Whalley Road, Manchester – Wednesday crashed 5-1 with an own goal from Rovers player Suter their only consolation on a forgettable day. An estimated crowd of 10,000 watched the action in only the tenth season of the relatively new tournament.

THURSDAY 15TH MARCH 1934

In a sensational move that shocked Owls fans, club captain and current England international Ernie Blenkinsop was sold to First Division rivals Liverpool, for a club record £6,500 fee. Fans who idolised Blenkinsop pointed the finger of blame at new manager Billy Walker who they believed saw the popular Blenkinsop as a threat to his own position.

THURSDAY 15th MARCH 1951

Wednesday smashed the British transfer record after paying Notts County £35,000 for inside-forward Jackie Sewell. It was hoped his talents would help Wednesday lift themselves out of the First Division relegation places but despite netting six times in ten games until the season's close, the Owls still went down.

SATURDAY 15th MARCH 1958

New signing Ron Springett was drafted straight into the side as struggling Wednesday beat Bolton Wanderers 1-0 (Albert Quixall) at Hillsborough to move out of the Division One relegation places.

TUESDAY 15th MARCH 1983

On an unforgettable night at Hillsborough, Wednesday beat fellow Second Division side Burnley 5-0 to march into the semi-finals of the FA Cup. Watched by 41,731 the Owls were 3-0 ahead at the interval – Gary Shelton (2) and a Gary Megson penalty – and a brace from Andy McCulloch wrapped up the eye-catching victory.

SATURDAY 16th MARCH 1895

In their fifth FA Cup semi-final, Wednesday suffered their fourth defeat, losing 2-0 to West Bromwich Albion in the last four meeting at the County Ground, Derby.

SATURDAY 16th MARCH 1918

Wednesday won 5-0 at Bramall Lane in a wartime game between the city rivals. Hero for Wednesday was Teddy Glennon who grabbed four goals in front of 12,000 fans.

SATURDAY 16th MARCH 1935

Due to a train delay and heavy traffic, the Owls did not arrive at Villa Park until 30 minutes before the start of their FA Cup semi-final against Burnley. They even had to complete the journey to the ground on foot but the poor preparation did not affect the side as they romped to a 3-0 win to reach Wembley for the first time. In front of a 56,625 crowd, goals from Ellis Rimmer (2) and Jack Palethorpe took Wednesday to their fourth final.

TUESDAY 16TH MARCH 1965

One of the greatest players in Wednesday's history, Ellis Rimmer, passed away in Formby, Lancashire. During his time at Wednesday he won four caps for England and won a multitude of honours after the Owls paid Tranmere Rovers £1,850 to obtain his signature in February 1928.

SATURDAY 17TH MARCH 1928

Wednesday continued to flounder at the foot of the First Division table, being cut adrift at the bottom by a seven-point margin after losing 4-2 at Bury – John Smith netting three for the Shakers.

WEDNESDAY 17TH MARCH 1993

A Paul Warhurst goal was enough to beat Derby County 1-0 at Hillsborough (32,033) to set up a dream FA Cup semi-final date with Sheffield United at Wembley.

SATURDAY 18TH MARCH 1939

While the Owls were beating West Bromwich Albion 2-1 at Hillsborough, a future manager of both teams, Ron Atkinson, was born in Liverpool. Without doubt one of the most charismatic and successful managers in the Owls' history, Atkinson was twice in charge at Hillsborough and led Wednesday to League Cup glory in 1991 before an acrimonious departure to boyhood club Aston Villa. He returned for a brief spell in 1997, helping the club to avoid relegation from the Premiership.

SATURDAY 18TH MARCH 2000

A disastrous 1-0 defeat to bottom club Watford, at Vicarage Road, marked the end of Danny Wilson's reign as manager. An 88th minute strike from Allan Smart deepened Wednesday woes at the foot of the Premiership.

SUNDAY 19TH MARCH 1899

Jack Brown was born in Worksop. The outstanding goalkeeper had not played football until the age of 17 but quickly rose to national prominence after helping his hometown club to a 0-0 FA Cup draw at Tottenham Hotspur in January 1923. He joined the Owls for £360 in February 1923 and won six full caps for England during over 14 years at Wednesday.

SATURDAY 19TH MARCH 1904

The top two sides in the First Division clashed at Goodison Park in the FA Cup semi-final. A crowd of 45,000 saw slight favourites Wednesday beaten 3-0 by an impressive Manchester City side that would win the trophy. Wednesday fans were not too impressed, though, after losing to a Lancashire club on a Lancashire ground in a game refereed by a Lancashire official!

SATURDAY 19TH MARCH 1927

Wednesday slumped to one of the heaviest defeats in their history as Derby County won 8-0 at the Baseball Ground in a top flight fixture. Jackie Whitehouse scored four and Harry Bedford three for County. It could have been worse for Wednesday as Whitehouse hit the crossbar and Gill had a seemingly good goal ruled out for a minor infringement!

SATURDAY 20TH MARCH 1897

The Owls played a friendly at renowned amateur side The Corinthians, Tommy Crawshaw and Harry Davis on target in a 2-1 win at the Queens Club.

SATURDAY 20TH MARCH 1937

A day after his 38th birthday, Jack Brown made his final first team appearance for the club with Wednesday losing 2-1 at home to Liverpool in front of 19,918 fans.

SATURDAY 21ST MARCH 1896

In the FA Cup semi-final at Goodison Park, 37,000 saw Wednesday grab a second-half equaliser through Archie Brash to force a replay against Bolton Wanderers, following a 1-1 draw.

WEDNESDAY 21ST MARCH 1956

The first Football League game played under floodlights at Hillsborough saw Division Two leaders Wednesday entertain Barnsley. A crowd of 31,577 saw a 3-0 win with Roy Shiner netting twice and Redfern Froggatt once.

MONDAY 21ST MARCH 1960

Born on this day in Sheffield, Mark Smith joined the Owls at the age of just 11 and came through the youth ranks to win England under-21 honours and help Wednesday to regain their top flight place lost in 1970.

SATURDAY 22ND MARCH 1930

There was huge controversy in the FA Cup semi-final against Huddersfield Town at Old Trafford. A crowd of 69,292 watched the Terriers recover from a Mark Hooper goal to lead 2-1 with seconds remaining. However, in one final attack Seed's pass found Jack Allen and the Wednesday man fired home an equaliser. The goal was disallowed as incredibly the referee blew for time as the ball was about to enter the net, ending the Owls' hopes of recording the first double of the 20th century.

TUESDAY 22ND MARCH 1994

The Owls made a midweek dash to Spain where they faced Real Madrid, in a game to officially open a new stadium in Cordoba. A crowd of 17,000 saw Real win 3-1 although a John Sheridan free kick provided the best goal of the game.

FRIDAY 23RD MARCH 1894

After failing to win an away game all season, the Owls recorded their second in a row; a Fred Spiksley goal enough to win 1-0 at Burnley in the penultimate game of the club's second season of league soccer.

SATURDAY 23RD MARCH 1907

In the FA Cup semi-final at St. Andrew's, Birmingham, Wednesday beat Woolwich Arsenal 3-1. A brace from centre-forward Andrew Wilson and a last-minute strike from Jimmy Stewart sent the Owls into their third final.

SATURDAY 23RD MARCH 1946

In the first FA Cup semi-final since VE Day, Birmingham City and Derby County drew 1-1 at Hillsborough – watched by a huge 65,013 gate.

SATURDAY 24TH MARCH 1900

Wombwell were put to the sword in a reserve game at Owlerton, Wednesday winning 16-0 with Jack Beech netting five goals.

MONDAY 24TH MARCH 1913

The Owls' title hopes remained alive after a 4-1 win at Derby County. Two goals each from George Robertson and David McLean gave Wednesday their eighth away win of the season.

SATURDAY 25th MARCH 1905

For the second consecutive season, Wednesday fell at the penultimate hurdle in the FA Cup as Jimmy Howie scored after 18 minutes for Newcastle United as they won 1-0 in the semi-final tie at Hyde Road, Manchester.

SATURDAY 25th MARCH 1978

The Owls continued their climb away from the foot of the Third Division, recording a terrific 2-1 win at neighbours Rotherham United – Jeff Johnson and Brian Hornsby netting.

SATURDAY 26th MARCH 1927

When the appointed linesman for the Wednesday v. Manchester United game failed to appear, Owls player Billy Felton ran the line as a replacement! A double from Jimmy Trotter clinched a 2-0 win for Wednesday although it is not known if the 'unbiased' linesman gave any contentious decisions!

SATURDAY 26th MARCH 1955

It was York City's greatest day. The Minstermen held top flight Newcastle United to a 1-1 draw at Hillsborough in the FA Cup semi-final, watched by 65,000 fans.

SATURDAY 26th MARCH 1960

The Owls faced Blackburn Rovers in the FA Cup semi-final at Maine Road, Manchester. In front of 74,135 the Lancashire side went into a two-goal lead thanks to a brace from Derek Dougan and despite John Fantham making the score 2-1 after 77 minutes the Owls could not force an equaliser.

SATURDAY 26th MARCH 1988

A 3-0 First Division win at Norwich City was illuminated by a wonder goal from Icelandic international Siggi Jonsson – the midfielder firing home from fully 35 yards. A Mel Sterland penalty and Lee Chapman goal completed the comfortable victory.

SATURDAY 27th MARCH 1954

In the FA Cup semi-final at Maine Road, the Owls held fellow First Division side Preston North End at the interval but the Lilywhites scored twice through Wayman and Baxter, in the second half, to earn a Wembley date with West Bromwich Albion.

FRIDAY 27TH MARCH 1959

It was not a good Friday for the Owls as promotion rivals Fulham beat them 6-2 in London with Jimmy Hill netting a hat-trick. Roy Shiner had levelled the game at 2-2 but Hill netted all his goals in the last fifteen minutes to somewhat flatter the hosts.

SATURDAY 27TH MARCH 1989

In a relegation clash at Newcastle United, Owls youngster Dean Barrick made a dream start as he scored just three minutes into his first-team debut. A 20-yard effort from David Hirst in the 90th minute sealed a 3-1 win.

SATURDAY 28TH MARCH 1896

At the Town Ground – home of Nottingham Forest – the Owls outplayed Bolton Wanderers in their FA Cup semi-final replay to win 3-1. In front of a poor crowd of under 10,000 goals from Tommy Crawshaw, Harry Davis and Fred Spiksley set up a final date with Wolves.

MONDAY 28TH MARCH 1932

On Easter Monday, the Owls beat visitors West Ham United 6-1 with Mark Hooper and Tom Jones scoring twice. The visitors had taken the lead after 25 minutes but Wednesday hit back to move up a place to third in the top flight.

WEDNESDAY 28TH MARCH 1962

A partisan 75,000 were at the Camp Nou to see Barcelona score twice in the first half to win 2-0 and send the Owls out of the Fairs Cup, 4-3 on aggregate.

TUESDAY 28TH MARCH 1972

A goalkeeping crisis resulted in amateur Trevor Pearson being called up for the game at Fulham. He was playing in the Sunday league for Woodseats WMC at the time but with the transfer deadline gone, Derek Dooley had no choice but to give the 19-year-old goalie a chance. Although the Owls lost 4-0 he was not at fault for any of the goals and played three more games before the injury problems eased.

SATURDAY 29TH MARCH 1890

The club's first appearance in an FA Cup final was a sobering experience as Blackburn Rovers won 6-1 in front of a 20,000 Kennington Oval crowd. Rovers were 4-0 ahead at half-time and despite a goal from Mickey Bennett (or Albert Mumford depending upon your source) there was no way back for Wednesday.

THURSDAY 29TH MARCH 1979

Manager Jack Charlton pulled off a real transfer market coup by signing Terry Curran from First Division Southampton for £85,000. In over three years at Wednesday, Curran became a huge crowd favourite, scoring 39 times in 138 games.

FRIDAY 29TH MARCH 2002

The only Good Friday game ever played in Sheffield took place on this day. Live TV coverage had seen the Wednesday v. Coventry City game put back from Saturday and with loan signings Kevin Gallacher and Jon McCarthy in the side, Wednesday registered a vital 2-1 win through a Gerald Sibon brace.

SATURDAY 30TH MARCH 1929

Wednesday maintained their First Division title challenge with a 4-2 win over Leeds United at Hillsborough. A hat-trick from winger Ellis Rimmer and one from skipper Jimmy Seed delighted the majority in the 30,655 crowd.

WEDNESDAY 30TH MARCH 1949

The club doctor, Andrew Stephen, was voted onto the board of directors. He was appointed chairman in May 1955 and became FA chairman in 1967 before being knighted for his services to football in June 1972.

TUESDAY 31ST MARCH 1891

The Owls met Glasgow Celtic for the first time, the Scots winning 3-1 at Olive Grove in front of 7,000. Wednesday took the lead through 'Toddles' Woolhouse after 20 minutes but the visitors quickly levelled.

SATURDAY 31ST MARCH 1973

Keeper Peter Fox became Wednesday's youngest-ever player, playing in the 2-0 home win over Orient at the age of 15 years, 8 months and 26 days.

SHEFFIELD WEDNESDAY
On This Day

APRIL

SATURDAY 1st APRIL 1876

The club played for the first time outside of England, losing 2-0 to Glasgow club Clydesdale in front of 7,000 fans.

TUESDAY 1st APRIL 1975

A 1-0 defeat at Nottingham Forest confirmed relegation to the Third Division for the first time. A penalty from George Lyall sealed the club's fate with five games still to be played.

SATURDAY 1st APRIL 1995

Unfortunately, it was no April Fools joke for Wednesday as Nottingham Forest beat them 7-1 at Hillsborough – the Owls' heaviest-ever home defeat. Stan Collymore and Stuart Pearce were among the scorers with a Mark Bright penalty a mere consolation for Wednesday in front of a stunned crowd in excess of 30,000.

SATURDAY 1st APRIL 2002

A minute's silence was held before the away game at Grimsby Town to mark the death of the Queen Mother, while Danny Maddix became the fifth Wednesday player to be red carded in the season, receiving a second yellow card in the first minute of the second half. A scrappy game ended 0-0 with both sides at the wrong end of the First Division table.

SATURDAY 2nd APRIL 1921

A Johnny McIntyre goal after 75 minutes gave Wednesday a 1-0 win against Stockport County at Edgeley Park. The mood of the home fans deteriorated throughout the game – the referee had awarded Wednesday two penalties on the previous Saturday – and at full time the officials locked themselves in the dressing rooms as stones and sticks were thrown by the angry mob!

SATURDAY 2nd APRIL 1994

Goals from Mark Bright (2), Ryan Jones, Chris Bart-Williams and Nigel Worthington gave Wednesday a resounding 5-1 home win over Everton in the Premiership.

WEDNESDAY 3rd APRIL 1912

Wednesday hosted their first FA Cup semi-final as a 20,050 midweek crowd saw West Bromwich Albion beat Blackburn Rovers 1-0 in a replayed tie.

SATURDAY 3RD APRIL 1993

Sheffield was like a ghost town as Wednesday met United at Wembley in the FA Cup semi-final. A wonder first-minute strike from Chris Waddle put the Owls ahead and with Alan Kelly inspired in goal for the Blades they held on to equalise through Alan Cork. It needed an extra time header from Mark Bright to settle the tie, sending Wednesday through.

THURSDAY 3RD APRIL 1997

Wednesday boss David Pleat was given a new improved contract, taking the former Luton Town manager through to June 2000. On the same day, shirt sponsors Sanderson signed a new improved deal, also through to the end of the 1999/00 season.

SATURDAY 4TH APRIL 1970

In a game relegation-threatened Wednesday desperately needed to win the Owls hit the woodwork, and had a Jack Whitham goal disallowed, before Everton winger Johnny Morrissey hit an 84th-minute winner.

SATURDAY 4TH APRIL 2009

The Owls recorded an eighth consecutive win against Norwich City; a goal from Jermaine Johnson secured a 1-0 Championship win at Carrow Road.

SATURDAY 5TH APRIL 1913

A fifth consecutive league win, 6-0 against Bradford City, left Wednesday top of the First Division with just four games to play. Goals from David McLean (2), Teddy Glennon, Sam Kirkman, Lawrie Burkinshaw and Percy Wright completed the rout.

SATURDAY 5TH APRIL 1930

England beat Scotland 5-2 at Wembley with Ellis Rimmer netting twice for his country. England also included Wednesday players Alf Strange, Billy Marsden and Ernie Blenkinsop. Meanwhile a depleted Wednesday side recorded a terrific 3-1 win at Liverpool to remain top of the First Division.

SATURDAY 5TH APRIL 1947

Coventry City centre-forward George Lowrie scored four times as the Owls were beaten 5-1 at Highfield Road. The defeat left Wednesday just one place off the relegation positions in the Second Division.

SATURDAY 5th APRIL 1986

A 52nd-minute equaliser from Carl Shutt took the FA Cup semi-final at Villa Park against Everton to extra time. The Toffeemen had taken the lead through future Owl Alan Harper and dashed Wednesday hopes of Wembley when Kevin Sheedy volleyed home the winner eight minutes into additional time. A crowd of 47,711 watched the Owls lose a semi-final for the second time in three years.

SATURDAY 6th APRIL 1895

After having officiated poorly in an Olive Grove fixture just two weeks previously, referee Mr. Lewis was barracked by Owls fans during the home game with Stoke. In the end the man in the middle decided to stop proceedings with fifteen minutes left and the score at 0-0. At this point a home fan ran onto the pitch and threw a grass sod at the referee – the missile missed Mr. Lewis but he abandoned the game and Wednesday found themselves in the Football League dock a few days later. They received a slap on the wrist and the game was replayed 11 days later with the visitors winning 4-2.

THURSDAY 6th APRIL 1961

Peter Shirtliff was born in the Sheffield suburb of Chapeltown. In two spells at Wednesday he recorded 359 appearances, the tenth highest tally for the Owls in post-war football.

SATURDAY 7th APRIL 1928

Wednesday's fight to escape the relegation places received a setback as Mark Hooper missed twice from the penalty spot in the 2-2 draw with Derby County at Hillsborough.

MONDAY 7th APRIL 1980

On Easter Monday, Wednesday stretched their unbeaten run in the Third Division to 15 games after a 1-0 home win over Gillingham, in front of almost 23,000 fans. A Mark Smith penalty after 73 minutes not only kept Wednesday firmly in the promotion hunt – second behind leaders Grimsby Town – but set a new club record of 11 successful spot kick conversions by Smith, beating the tally set by Jack Ball back in the 1930s.

SUNDAY 8TH APRIL 1934

Trainer Chris Craig died just over a month after he had been taken ill before the Sheffield derby at Bramall Lane. The outstanding coach had initially joined Wednesday as assistant to George Utley in 1924 and was promoted to senior trainer a year later.

FRIDAY 8TH APRIL 1955

Despite gaining a 2-2 draw at Bolton Wanderers, the Owls were relegated on Good Friday, with still five games remaining to play. The only two teams that Wednesday could have caught – Blackpool and Newcastle United – both won to send Wednesday back down to the Second Division.

SATURDAY 8TH APRIL 1967

Wednesday suffered late heartbreak when Chelsea scored the only goal of the game in injury time to win an FA Cup sixth-round tie at Stamford Bridge, in front of 52,481.

SATURDAY 9TH APRIL 1927

Only 9,020 were at Hillsborough to see goals from Jimmy Trotter, Mark Hooper and Alf Strange beat Aston Villa 3-1. The game saw the debut of new attacker Jack Allen who had joined from Brentford for £750 the previous month.

SATURDAY 9TH APRIL 1938

In a proverbial 'six pointer' a goal from Doug Hunt sealed a vital 1-0 win at fellow strugglers Nottingham Forest. The two points enabled Wednesday to move out of the bottom two and leapfrog their opponents.

MONDAY 9TH APRIL 1962

One of the greatest players in Wednesday's history passed away in Sheffield. The 507 appearances registered by Jack Brown meant he was one of only three men to pass the 500-game mark for the club.

SATURDAY 10TH APRIL 1920

In an incredible clash between the 'auld enemy' England beat Scotland 5-4 at Hillsborough, in the first full international staged by Wednesday. The only Owls player on show was in the Scottish ranks, Jimmy Blair winning the second of his two caps earned whilst at Hillsborough.

SATURDAY 10TH APRIL 1926

In a crucial game at the top of the Second Division, a crowd of 41,817 were inside Stamford Bridge to see goalkeeper Jack Brown save Barrett's 88th-minute penalty to earn Wednesday a vital point.

SATURDAY 10TH APRIL 1965

Future Owl, John Ritchie, grabbed four goals as Wednesday were beaten 4-1 at Stoke City, watched by 16,047.

MONDAY 11TH APRIL 1921

FA Cup finalists Wolverhampton Wanderers were beaten 6-0 at Hillsborough. The visitors clearly had the final on their minds as goals from Sam Taylor (2), Jimmy Lofthouse, Johnny McIntyre, Jack Smelt and Arthur Price gave Wednesday the points.

SATURDAY 11TH APRIL 1998

The only top flight Oakwell meeting between Barnsley and Wednesday resulted in a 2-1 win for the Tykes. The Owls gave a debut to virtual unknown Emerson Thome – just over 18 months later the Brazilian was sold to Chelsea for £2.5m, after 71 games for Wednesday, and later commanded a £4.5m fee when he moved to Sunderland.

SATURDAY 12TH APRIL 1890

The Wednesday beat Sunderland Albion 4-1 at Olive Grove, for a 100% home record in the Alliance League. Exactly 50 goals were scored – averaging over four per game – as Wednesday walked the inaugural championship.

SUNDAY 12TH APRIL 1964

Revelations in the *Sunday People* newspaper implicated several footballers in a betting scandal with two Wednesday players (Peter Swan and Bronco Layne) and one ex-Owl (Tony Kay) featuring prominently in the story.

SATURDAY 12TH APRIL 2003

Bottom side Wednesday played the role of 'party poopers' at Fratton Park as Portsmouth looked for the win to clinch promotion to the Premiership. The party looked set to start when Lee Bradbury put Pompey in front after 20 minutes but Ashley Westwood equalised and with virtually the last kick of the game Michael Reddy ran through to fire home a dramatic winner.

SATURDAY 13TH APRIL 1929

Wednesday nudged ever closer to the First Division championship as West Ham United were beaten 6-0 at Hillsborough with Alf Strange and Mark Hooper grabbing two goals apiece.

MONDAY 13TH APRIL 1964

The home game with Spurs was dominated by the breaking story of the bribes scandal. Goals from Derek Wilkinson gave Wednesday a 2-0 win while at half-time secretary-manager Eric Taylor gave a stirring speech, asking the fans to "be patient with the club in its time of trouble". The club announced that Layne and Swan had been suspended with immediate effect.

SUNDAY 13TH APRIL 1986

A live ITV audience watched on as Wednesday completed the double over Manchester United, winning 2-0 at Old Trafford thanks to a low drive from Carl Shutt and a Mel Sterland penalty.

SATURDAY 14TH APRIL 1928

A double from Jack Allen clinched a 2-1 win at West Ham to lift the Owls off the bottom of the table for the first time since Boxing Day. Wednesday nudged ahead of Sheffield United on goal average with fans now starting to believe that the 'great escape' was a possibility.

TUESDAY 14TH APRIL 1959

A goal from Red Froggatt after 65 minutes was enough to beat visitors Liverpool and secure the club's fourth promotion from the Second Division in the 1950s.

SATURDAY 14TH APRIL 1984

In a crucial top-of-the-table game at Newcastle United, a spectacular overhead kick from Gary Shelton settled a drab match, leaving the Owls just three wins from promotion.

SATURDAY 15TH APRIL 1899

The visit of Newcastle United marked the end of the Olive Grove era in the club's history. After twelve seasons, 4,000 fans said goodbye with Bob Hutton scoring the last ever goal from an Owls player as the Geordies won 3-1. The defeat also confirmed the club's relegation from the top flight.

SATURDAY 15TH APRIL 1989

On a terrible day for English football the FA Cup semi-final between Liverpool and Nottingham Forest was abandoned after six minutes due to overcrowding in the Leppings Lane end, causing fatalities. The final death toll reached 96 with the tragedy changing the face of English football forever.

SATURDAY 16TH APRIL 1983

Wednesday lost 2-1 to First Division Brighton & Hove Albion in the FA Cup semi-final at Highbury. Watched by 54,627, Ante Mirocevic pulled the Owls level after 57 minutes but Michael Robinson hit the winner for the Seagulls after 77 minutes.

SATURDAY 17TH APRIL 1920

The Owls lost 3-1 at Aston Villa, despite leading through Jimmy Gill, to confirm their relegation from the First Division, with four games left.

MONDAY 17TH APRIL 1961

Thousands of fans were locked out of White Hart Lane as 61,200 saw Spurs beat their nearest challengers, Wednesday, 2-1 to win the league title.

TUESDAY 17TH APRIL 1984

Pre war hero Jimmy Trotter died in St. Albans. He was a huge favourite with Wednesday fans with the song "Trot, Trot, Trotter, score a little goal for me" often heard reverberating around the terraces.

MONDAY 17TH APRIL 2006

Three years after Wednesday were relegated at Brighton on Easter Monday, the Owls returned to seal the fate of the Seagulls. An own goal from Gary Hart, and a solo strike by Burton O'Brien in the 69th minute, confirmed relegation for Albion, Crewe and Millwall.

SATURDAY 18TH APRIL 1896

A goal inside the first two minutes from Fred Spiksley gave Wednesday the lead in the FA Cup final at Crystal Palace. Wolves equalised soon after but the crowd of 48,836 in the capital saw Spiksley net his second after 20 minutes and that proved enough as the Owls won 2-1 to lift the trophy for the first time.

BURTON O'BRIEN, SCORER AT BRIGHTON & HOVE ALBION IN APRIL 2006, UNDER A MASS OF BODIES

SATURDAY 18TH APRIL 1903

In Fred Spiksley's last game, a 3-1 victory over West Bromwich Albion left Wednesday as champions elect with the only team able to catch them, Sunderland, still having a game left to play.

SUNDAY 18TH APRIL 1993

In front of a 74,007 crowd, the Owls scored first in the League Cup final against Arsenal – John Harkes becoming the first American to score in a major final at Wembley. However, the Gunners hit back through Paul Merson and Steve Morrow to lift the trophy.

SATURDAY 19TH APRIL 1952

Thanks to two goals from the irrepressible Derek Dooley, Wednesday won 2-0 at Coventry City to not only seal promotion back to the top flight but also the Second Division title.

SATURDAY 19TH APRIL 1975

Only 7,444 attended the 1-1 home draw against Oxford United but the loyal few were rewarded as Brian Joicey scored in the 89th minute – the Owls' first goal at home since December 14th 1974, a span of 14 hours and 25 minutes! A fan remarked; "I was glad I was there to see that goal. I shall tell my grandchildren in years to come that I was there for that one."

SUNDAY 20TH APRIL 1902

Probably the club's finest left-back, Ernest Blenkinsop, was born in Cudworth, Barnsley. He notched up 424 games for Wednesday between 1923 and 1934, winning 26 England caps.

SATURDAY 20TH APRIL 1907

It was cup final day as 84,500 fans squeezed into the Crystal Palace ground at Sydenham, London for the meeting between Wednesday and Everton. A Jimmy Stewart goal made the score 1-1 but with just four minutes remaining the Owls launched an attack and George Simpson headed home the winner, delighting the travelling Wednesday fans.

MONDAY 20TH APRIL 1931

A 6pm evening kick-off meant only 5,141 were inside Hillsborough to see Wednesday come back twice to beat Derby County 3-2.

SATURDAY 20TH APRIL 1974

Wednesday remained in Second Division relegation trouble after Jack Charlton's runaway leaders Middlesbrough won 8-0 with Graeme Souness netting three.

TUESDAY 20TH APRIL 1976

In a terrible season, a Phil Henson goal was enough to beat Halifax Town at Hillsborough. The vital win was Wednesday's fourth 1-0 home victory in a row, a run of form that would ultimately prove their saviour.

SATURDAY 21ST APRIL 1923

New signing Jack Brown made his first team bow as Wednesday drew 1-1 at Coventry City in the Second Division. A crowd of 12,000 were at Highfield Road with Fred Kean equalising after 29 minutes to earn a point.

SATURDAY 21ST APRIL 1956

In front of 23,333, Wednesday won 5-2 at Bury to not only clinch promotion back to the top flight but also secure the Second Division championship. Scorers for the Owls were Roy Shiner (2), Albert Broadbent, Alan Finney and Albert Quixall.

SUNDAY 21ST APRIL 1991

On an unforgettable day at Wembley, underdogs Wednesday won the League Cup after beating Manchester United 1-0. A sweet strike from John Sheridan after 37 minutes won the trophy for Wednesday in front of 77,612 fans. Captain Nigel Pearson lifted the club's first major trophy since 1935 – his five goals in the competition being instrumental in the success.

SATURDAY 21ST APRIL 2001

Wednesday beat Barnsley 2-1 at Hillsborough. Goals from Gerald Sibon and Simon Donnelly ended any lingering relegation worries. The game was also Des Walker's last in a Wednesday shirt – finances dictated that the club could not offer the Player of the Season a new deal so he left after 362 games.

SUNDAY 21ST APRIL 2002

The Owls drew 2-2 against promotion hopefuls Wolves at Hillsborough on the final day. Almost 30,000 were inside the ground to see the Owls earn the point required to guarantee their First Division survival.

MONDAY 21ST APRIL 2003

It was a miserable Easter for Wednesday fans as their side could only draw 1-1 at Brighton. With relegation rivals Stoke City winning at Coventry City the Owls were relegated to the third tier of the English game for only the second time.

TUESDAY 22ND APRIL 1930

With four games remaining, Wednesday retained their First Division crown after beating nearest rivals Derby County 6-3 at Hillsborough. In front of 41,218 fans, Wednesday raced into a 6-0 lead after an hour with a hat-trick from top scorer Jack Allen and goals from Harry Millership, Mark Hooper and Ellis Rimmer.

WEDNESDAY 22ND APRIL 1970

A seasonal best crowd of 45,258 packed Hillsborough in the hope of spurring Wednesday to the win needed against Manchester City to save the club from relegation. Unfortunately, it was not to be – despite Tony Coleman equalising an Ian Bowyer goal – the visitors won 2-1 to send the Owls down into the Second Division.

TUESDAY 22ND APRIL 1980

Wednesday beat promotion rivals Blackburn Rovers 2-1 at Ewood Park in a crucial Third Division game. They were behind at the break but an equaliser from Kevin Taylor and an 82nd-minute winner from Ian Mellor sent the huge 10,000-strong away following, in the 26,130 crowd, home happy.

SUNDAY 23RD APRIL 1882

Once described as "the perfect footballer", Tom Brittleton was born in Winsford, Cheshire. In a Wednesday career that lasted fifteen years he scored 33 goals in 372 games for the club, in addition to 10 goals in 129 games during the Great War.

SATURDAY 23RD APRIL 1910

The meeting of two mid-table sides at the City Ground provided an unlikely score as Wednesday beat Nottingham Forest 6-0 in the penultimate game of the season. Only 5,000 attended the game as the Owls recorded one of the biggest away wins in their history.

SATURDAY 23RD APRIL 1966

Wednesday rose to the occasion to beat Chelsea 2-0 in the FA Cup semi-final on a mudbath of a pitch at Villa Park. Watched by 61,321, Wednesday took the lead through Graham Pugh after 55 minutes and ex-Chelsea attacker Jim McCalliog sealed the trip to Wembley when he headed home the second in the final minute.

SATURDAY 23RD APRIL 1988

The infamous plastic pitch at Queens Park Rangers hosted league football for the last time as Wednesday drew 1-1 at Loftus Road. At the end of the game, home fans ran onto the surface and started to rip up parts of the pitch to take home as souvenirs!

SATURDAY 24TH APRIL 1926

Promotion back into the First Division was confirmed. Two goals from Jimmy Trotter saw the Owls come from a goal down to win 2-1 at Southampton.

THURSDAY 24TH APRIL 1969

Whilst serving a customer at his Crosspool public house, Ernie Blenkinsop collapsed and died, aged 67. A week earlier he had won his golf club's championship to ensure he would always be remembered as a winner.

SATURDAY 25TH APRIL 1903

With Wednesday having already finished their First Division fixtures, they beat Notts County 2-0 in a friendly played at Plymouth. After being presented with the Plymouth Bowl there were further celebrations when news filtered through that title rivals Sunderland had lost to Newcastle United – confirming Wednesday as champions for the first time.

MONDAY 25TH APRIL 1904

Wednesday were crowned champions for the second successive season as nearest rivals Manchester City lost 1-0 at Everton in their final league game.

SATURDAY 25TH APRIL 1959

The Owls clinched the Second Division title after beating Barnsley 5-0 at Hillsborough. Red Froggatt and Roy Shiner both scored twice as 17,917 celebrated the fourth time that Wednesday had immediately bounced back into the top flight following relegation.

SATURDAY 25TH APRIL 1981

Incredibly, a heavy fall of snow caused the home game with West Ham United to be postponed – the latest date a first team game has fallen victim to the British weather.

SATURDAY 25TH APRIL 1992

Any outside championship hopes ended when Mark Bright netted an 88th-minute equaliser for Crystal Palace in the 1-1 draw at Selhurst Park. However, any disappointment soon turned to joy as results elsewhere meant Wednesday had qualified for the Uefa Cup.

SATURDAY 26TH APRIL 1890

The 22nd and final Football Alliance League game of the season: Wednesday won 2-1 at Newton Heath; a 15th win which clinched the championship.

WEDNESDAY 26TH APRIL 1905

The 1904/05 season ended with a 3-1 home defeat to Newcastle United. Stalwart Bob Ferrier made his final appearance after 12 seasons as an Owl.

SATURDAY 26TH APRIL 1958

Wednesday beat Wolves 2-1 at Hillsborough in the final game of the 1957/58 season. Goals from Derek Wilkinson and Roy Shiner secured the win against the newly crowned league champions but Wednesday finished 22nd and last, suffering their third relegation of the decade.

WEDNESDAY 26TH APRIL 1961

The Owls dominated at Stamford Bridge to win 2-0 against Chelsea to secure the First Division runners-up spot behind double winners Tottenham.

SATURDAY 26TH APRIL 1980

Defeat for promotion rivals Chesterfield, at Millwall, meant the Owls were celebrating promotion from the third tier, despite losing 1-0 at Exeter City.

SATURDAY 26TH APRIL 2003

Wednesday won 7-2 at Burnley – the club's biggest-ever league away win. In a game that saw all four goalkeepers take the field, the Owls had seven different scorers – Paul McLaren, Ashley Westwood, Richard Wood, Richard Evans, Steve Haslam, Alan Quinn and a Gnohere own goal.

SATURDAY 26TH APRIL 2008

A vital 3-1 win at Leicester boosted the Owls' Championship survival hopes. Both sides missed from the penalty spot but goals from Bartosz Slusarski, Steve Watson and Leon Clarke sealed the win.

SATURDAY 27TH APRIL 1912

A 5-1 win at West Bromwich Albion secured fifth place in the First Division. Centre-forward David McLean took his seasonal tally in the league to 25 with a treble and Sam Kirkman grabbed a brace.

SATURDAY 27TH APRIL 1929

The Owls were crowned champions of England – with a points tally of 52 – after a 1-1 home draw with Burnley. A header after 81 minutes from Jack Allen claimed the required point as nearest rivals Leicester City could only draw.

SATURDAY 27TH APRIL 1935

Wednesday beat West Bromwich Albion 4-2 in the FA Cup final at Wembley. A 93,204 crowd saw four goals shared between Jack Palethorpe and Mark Hooper before Ellis Rimmer scored twice in the last three minutes – setting a new record of having scored in every round of the competition.

TUESDAY 27TH APRIL 1954

In a Sheffield County Cup tie with Rotherham United at Hillsborough, Wednesday led 3-0 after just 25 minutes but somehow lost the match 5-3!

SATURDAY 27TH APRIL 1974

There were joyous scenes at Hillsborough as captain Ken Knighton was chaired off the field by fans after scoring the vital goal that saved the Owls from relegation into the third tier of the English game. His 85th-minute strike was the only goal of the game against Bolton Wanderers, watched by a relieved 23,264 crowd.

SATURDAY 28TH APRIL 1900

Goals from Harry Davis (2) and Jack Pryce secured a 3-0 Owlerton win over Middlesbrough. The last-day victory meant that in winning the Second Division championship they posted a 100% home record, winning all 17 fixtures, with a 61-7 goals tally.

SATURDAY 28TH APRIL 1984

A Mel Sterland penalty was enough to beat Crystal Palace at Hillsborough and clinch promotion to the top flight, 14 years after being relegated.

SATURDAY 28TH APRIL 2001

It was a 'Honolulu Wednesday' away day at Norwich City with Owls fans adorned in Hawaiian shirts, straw hats, grass skirts and Bermuda shorts!

SATURDAY 29TH APRIL 1939

Wednesday finished their season in the second promotion place after a Charlie Napier goal beat Tottenham Hotspur 1-0 at Hillsborough. However, city rivals United beat Spurs 6-1 in their game in hand to deny the Owls promotion.

THURSDAY 29TH APRIL 1976

Wednesday beat Southend United 2-1 at Hillsborough to avoid the drop into Division Four. Goals from Mick Prendergast and Eric Potts sealed the win in front of 25,802 supporters.

SATURDAY 29TH APRIL 1978

In the penultimate game of the campaign, Wednesday handed a debut to 18-year-old Mark Smith for the trip to Colchester United. The hosts took the lead and Chris Turner then saved a penalty kick before Dave Rushbury rescued a point in the second half.

SATURDAY 30TH APRIL 1892

Wednesday played their final game as a non-league club – a 0-0 friendly against Derby County at Olive Grove. The term 'friendly' was inappropriate, though, as both Jim Brandon (Wednesday) and Archie Goodall (Derby) were sent off after a small disagreement!

SATURDAY 30TH APRIL 1960

Wednesday drew 1-1 at West Ham United, in Red Froggatt's farewell game, on the final day of the season, to finish fifth in the First Division.

SATURDAY 30TH APRIL 2005

A scrappy last-minute goal from James Quinn sealed a crucial 2-1 win at Hull City to cement the Owls' place in the League One play-offs.

SHEFFIELD WEDNESDAY
On This Day

MAY

SATURDAY 1st MAY 1920

The Owls brought the desperate 1919/20 season to a close with a 1-0 home win over Oldham Athletic, an 89th-minute effort from William Taylor earning the points. The game had extra significance, however, as veteran Tom Brittleton made his final appearance for Wednesday at the grand old age of 38 years, 8 days – making him one of the oldest players to wear the blue and white shirt.

SATURDAY 1st MAY 1926

Jimmy Trotter's 37th league goal of the season set the Owls on their way to a 2-0 home win over Blackpool that secured the Second Division championship. Darkie Lowdell grabbed the second with the fans invading the pitch at the final whistle to celebrate promotion back to the top flight after a six-year absence.

SATURDAY 1st MAY 1937

Wednesday travelled to Huddersfield Town needing a win and other results to go their way if relegation was to be avoided. Unfortunately, the various permutations were not required as the Terriers won 1-0 to confirm relegation to the Second Division.

SATURDAY 1st MAY 1965

In front of 70,000 fans in Katowice, Wednesday lost 2-1 to a brace from Jarosik for a Polish Select XI side.

WEDNESDAY 1st MAY 1991

Wednesday's under-18 side appeared in their first-ever FA Youth Cup final, losing 3-0 at Hillsborough in the first leg of the final to Millwall. Some pride was restored a week later when the second game ended 0-0 at the Den.

SATURDAY 2nd MAY 1913

A bumper 16,000 crowd was inside Hillsborough to see Sheffield boys beat West Ham boys 1-0 to lift the prestigious English Schools Trophy.

WEDNESDAY 2nd MAY 1928

In the most amazing finish to any top flight season, the bottom four teams all had the same points after a dramatic last-minute goal from Wednesday captain Jimmy Seed earned a 1-1 draw at Arsenal.

SATURDAY 2ND MAY 1970

Wednesday played their first game in the new Anglo-Italian tournament, beating Napoli 4-3 at Hillsborough in front of 10,166 fans. Two goals each from Steve Downes and Alan Warboys had seen the Owls 4-0 ahead but three goals in the second half from the visitors left Wednesday hanging on at the end.

SATURDAY 2ND MAY 1987

In a First Division game at Hillsborough, the Owls overwhelmed Queens Park Rangers, winning 7-1, hitting the woodwork twice and having an eighth goal bizarrely not given by the referee although the visiting goalkeeper was stood behind the goal-line with the ball in his hands! David Hirst and Brian Marwood led the way with a brace apiece while Gary Megson, Mel Sterland and Mark Chamberlain completed the rout.

SATURDAY 3RD MAY 1930

The most successful season in the club's history came to a close in fine style as Manchester City were beaten 5-1 at Hillsborough, in front of 22,293 fans. A treble from Mark Hooper made him second-top scorer for the season with 21 although slightly behind outstanding centre-forward Jack Allen who finished with 39 goals to his name. The Owls' tally of sixty points equalled the league record while a goal haul of 105 was the highest amount ever scored by a league championship-winning side. Both records lasted a year before being smashed by Arsenal!

WEDNESDAY 3RD MAY 1933

In the second game of the club's mini tour to southern Ireland, Wednesday beat Shelbourne 4-1 in front of 15,000 fans at Dalymount Park, Dublin.

SATURDAY 3RD MAY 1978

Third Division champions Wrexham were beaten at Hillsborough in the final game of the 1977-78 campaign. The second-best league crowd of the season, 15,700, gave the Owls a great send off as goals from Brian Hornsby (penalty) and Tommy Tynan clinched a 2-1 win.

SATURDAY 3rd MAY 1986

A Brian Marwood goal after 82 minutes was enough to beat Ipswich Town in the last game played at Hillsborough before the Kop was covered. The win ensured Wednesday finished the season in fifth place but the post Heysel European ban meant the club missed out on Uefa Cup football.

WEDNESDAY 4th MAY 1921

With women's football in England at its peak of popularity, the famous Dick Kerr's Ladies visited Hillsborough. A 22,000 crowd watched them beat a Yorkshire side called Atalanta 4-0.

SATURDAY 4th MAY 1935

Wednesday completed their First Division programme – and unbeaten home record - with a 1-0 win over Grimsby Town, taking the club to a final finishing position of third. The Owls ran out with the freshly won FA Cup in their hands – to a huge reception – and manager Billy Walker paraded around the ground at the interval so fans could touch the famous old trophy.

SATURDAY 4th MAY 1985

An outstanding goalkeeping display from Neville Southall left the Owls frustrated as champions-elect Everton won 1-0 at Hillsborough, in the penultimate home game of the 1984/85 season. A crowd of 37,381 watched the game in a season when Wednesday's home average was 27,779.

SUNDAY 4th MAY 2008

The highest crowd of the season in the Championship (36,208) filled Hillsborough to see Wednesday go behind to visitors Norwich City. A brilliant save from Lee Grant denied the Canaries a second goal and Wednesday then found their shooting boots to win 4-1 (Deon Burton (2), Ben Sahar and Leon Clarke) to retain Championship status.

SATURDAY 5th MAY 1928

Wednesday completed the 'great escape' by beating Aston Villa 2-0 at Hillsborough in front of a jubilant 36,636 crowd. Goals from Jack Allen and Jimmy Trotter meant Wednesday had won eight of their final twelve games to finish 14th.

SATURDAY 5TH MAY 1951

Wednesday required at least a 6-0 win from their final game of the season at home to Everton to have any chance of avoiding relegation. Incredibly, in front of 41,166 they did win 6-0 but sadly relegation rivals Chelsea won 4-0 so the Owls toppled out of the division in the same way as they had been promoted a year earlier – on goal average.

SUNDAY 5TH MAY 1957

An Owls youth side beat MVV Maastricht 2-1 to win the Voellkingen Youth Tournament in Germany. It was the first time the Owls had competed abroad at youth level with John Fantham and B. Finney scoring the goals.

WEDNESDAY 5TH MAY 1965

The Owls finished their mini tour of Poland with a 1-0 defeat to a Warsaw Select XI, watched by 15,000 fans.

SATURDAY 5TH MAY 1990

Despite only needing a point to guarantee First Division safety, Wednesday lost 3-0 at home to Nottingham Forest in front of a disbelieving 29,762 crowd. The result took the issue out of the club's hands and news duly filtered through that Luton Town had won at Derby County and Wednesday were down with neighbours United taking their place in the top division.

MONDAY 6TH MAY 1935

The Owls met Grimsby Town in a benefit match for the local fishermen. Wednesday took the FA Cup with them and boosted the funds by allowing fans to touch the trophy for sixpence – at the time it was considered lucky to touch the cup. The Mariners won 3-1, watched by a bumper 18,000 crowd.

SATURDAY 6TH MAY 1950

In a dramatic end to the season, 50,853 fans were at Hillsborough to see the Owls hang on to a nervous 0-0 draw against Second Division champions Tottenham. The draw meant the Owls pipped the Blades to the second promotion spot by a better goal average (goals scored/goals conceded) of just 0.008!

SATURDAY 6TH MAY 1967

The Owls crushed Burnley 7-0 at Hillsborough with David Ford (3), Jack Whitman (2), Jim McCalliog and John Quinn finding the net. Whitham, a half-time sub, became the first Wednesday player to score from the bench.

SUNDAY 6TH MAY 2007

A last-day Hillsborough crowd of 28,287 saw the Owls beat visitors Norwich City 3-2 and end a season where the club had just missed out on the play offs, finishing four points away in ninth.

SATURDAY 7TH MAY 1938

Goals from Doug Hunt and Bill Fallon clinched a 2-1 win at Spurs to save the club from relegation to Division Three (North) football. Despite Hunt missing a penalty and Tottenham pulling a goal back the Owls held on to avoid the drop.

SATURDAY 7TH MAY 1988

League champions Liverpool gave the Owls a football lesson on the final day of the 1987/88 campaign winning 5-1 at Hillsborough with Peter Beardsley (2), Craig Johnston (2) and John Barnes scoring for the visitors, and David Hirst grabbing a late consolation goal for Wednesday.

SATURDAY 7TH MAY 1994

The Owls drew 1-1 with Manchester City on the final day of the season. It was also the farewell appearance of outstanding right-back Roland Nilsson, who returned home to Sweden after three goals in 186 appearances. The match also proved to be the last appearance of long-serving left-back Nigel Worthington, who re-joined old boss Howard Wilkinson at Leeds United, after 417 appearances.

SATURDAY 8TH MAY 1965

In sunny Spain, the Owls lost 3-0 to Valencia in a friendly, played in Madrid.

SATURDAY 8TH MAY 1982

A 3-1 defeat at Bolton Wanderers, in the last away game of the season, ended the Owls' hopes of earning promotion to the top flight. They had led through Terry Curran after only four minutes but the home side hit back.

WEDNESDAY 8TH MAY 1991

The Owls beat Bristol City 3-1 at Hillsborough to clinch promotion from the Second Division, watched by 31,706. A David Hirst goal after 35 minutes calmed any nerves and the promotion party went into full swing as Trevor Francis (54) and Hirst again (64) wrapped up a league and cup double.

SATURDAY 8TH MAY 1993

In their penultimate Premiership fixture of the season, Wednesday lost 1-0 at Blackburn Rovers to slide a place to sixth. The game also proved to be Peter Shirtliff's final game for the Owls as injury would deny the centre-half a farewell appearance at Wembley in the FA Cup final.

SATURDAY 8TH MAY 2004

A large travelling contingent of QPR fans swelled the crowd to 29,313 on the season's final day. The Londoners went home happy as they were promoted following a 3-1 win. An own goal from Chris Carr completed the scoring in Kevin Pressman's final appearance in an Owls shirt. The defeat meant the Owls finished 16th in Division Two – the second-worst finish in the club's history.

SUNDAY 9TH MAY 1954

The Owls met Sao Paulo club Portuguesa Desportes in Antwerp, Belgium and were given a real football lesson by the Brazilians losing 6-0. Wednesday manager Eric Taylor admitted that the crowd had been treated to "football at its finest".

SATURDAY 9TH MAY 1987

The Wimbledon 'crazy gang' ruined the Owls' final game of the season as they won 2-0 at Hillsborough. When Howard Wilkinson substituted Mark Smith after 68 minutes it brought the curtain down on nine years as a professional with Wednesday. Smith later worked as an Academy coach at both Wednesday and Sheffield United.

WEDNESDAY 9TH MAY 1989

In the first game played at Hillsborough since the semi-final disaster, the Owls lost 2-0 to West Ham United to further deepen the club's relegation worries.

TUESDAY 9TH MAY 2000

Wednesday were just nine minutes away from a win at Highbury, which would have taken the relegation battle to the final day of the season. Unfortunately, the Gunners scored twice inside a minute to rescue a 3-3 draw and condemn Wednesday to the First Division.

SATURDAY 10TH MAY 1930

The Owls provided four players for England as they drew 3-3 with Germany, in Berlin, in the first full international between the countries. Ernest Blenkinsop, Alf Strange, Ellis Rimmer and Billy Marsden were the Wednesday men in question although for Marsden it would be a sad day as he was so seriously injured in the game that his career was ended prematurely.

TUESDAY 10TH MAY 1961

The Owls opened their tour of Nigeria with a comprehensive 11-2 win over Western Nigeria in Ibadan – Gerry Young netting five for Wednesday.

MONDAY 10TH MAY 1965

At Dalymount Park, Dublin, John Hickton scored twice as the Owls beat Shamrock Rovers 4-3 in a close season exhibition game.

SUNDAY 10TH MAY 1998

Wednesday lost 1-0 to an injury-time strike from Crystal Palace youngster Clinton Morrison on the final day of the Premiership season. The game proved to be the final one of Ron Atkinson's second spell in charge at Wednesday.

FRIDAY 11TH MAY 1979

Goals from Brian Hornsby and Ian Nimmo secured a 2-1 Hillsborough win over Swindon Town. The game was one of six Third Division matches played in 19 days in a congested end to the season.

SATURDAY 11TH MAY 1991

Wednesday looked to end the glorious 1990/91 season with a win on Oldham Athletic's notorious 'plastic pitch'. Goals from David Hirst and Danny Wilson put the Owls 2-0 ahead after 51 minutes but the Latics stormed back to win 3-2 and snatch the title from West Ham United – a last minute penalty from Neil Redfearn clinching the win.

SATURDAY 11TH MAY 1997

On the final day, Wednesday drew 1-1 against Liverpool, O'Neill Donaldson scoring for the Owls. The talking point though occurred before the game kicked off when a rather buxom young lady streaked across the pitch! The stunt was organised by a leading men's magazine and the scenario was repeated at all of the day's Premiership games.

MONDAY 12TH MAY 1969

Wednesday ended the season with a 0-0 draw against visitors Tottenham Hotspur. Highlight of the evening for the 28,368 crowd was the debut of teenager Tommy Craig who would appear in 233 games for Wednesday over the next five years, scoring 40 goals.

SATURDAY 12TH MAY 1984

The race for the Second Division championship was decided on the final day as the Owls won 2-0 at Cardiff City. Despite news filtering through that Chelsea had won to take the title there were still carnival scenes at the end with the Wednesday fans singing "we're proud of you" to their side.

THURSDAY 12TH MAY 2005

The Owls' first experience of the play-off system saw an 11th-minute goal from J. P. McGovern beat Brentford 1-0 in the first leg of the semi-final, in front of 28,625 at Hillsborough.

TUESDAY 13TH MAY 1952

In the first game played by Wednesday under floodlights, they drew 2-2 with a Bellinzona Select XI during a five-game tour of Switzerland.

THURSDAY 13TH MAY 1954

Under the Paris floodlights, Wednesday won 5-3 in a thrilling game against Bangu, from Rio de Janeiro. The Owls netted through Jack Shaw (3), Red Froggatt and Dennis Woodhead with Norman Curtis missing a penalty.

SATURDAY 13TH MAY 1989

In a 'winner takes all' clash at Hillsborough, Wednesday beat Middlesbrough 1-0 to save themselves from relegation from Division One and send their Teesside visitors down – a Steve Whitton header from a succession of corners proved enough.

SATURDAY 14TH MAY 1966

The club's fifth FA Cup final appearance proved bittersweet as Wednesday led 2-0 at Wembley through goals from Jim McCalliog after four minutes and David Ford after 57 minutes. However, the 100,000 crowd then saw virtual unknown Mike Trebilcock score twice to level matters before Derek Temple hit the winner for Everton after 72 minutes.

SUNDAY 14TH MAY 1995

Wednesday ended the 1994/95 season on a high, beating Ipswich Town 4-1 at Hillsborough to banish any relegation fears. Despite the win, the game proved to be manager Trevor Francis' last game as Owls boss.

WEDNESDAY 15TH MAY 1963

In the Sheffield derby, Wednesday trailed to a Doc Pace goal at the break but came back to win 3-1 with Bronco Layne (2) and Tom McAnearney scoring in front of 41,585 at Hillsborough.

MONDAY 15TH MAY 1967

The Owls ended the season with a 1-0 defeat to Leeds United at Elland Road. The game was the last for club legend Ron Springett who after 384 games and 33 caps for England returned home to London.

SATURDAY 15TH MAY 1993

Arsenal led through Ian Wright's 21st-minute goal but David Hirst equalised after 62 minutes as Wednesday and Arsenal drew 1-1 in the FA Cup final at Wembley. Thirty minutes of extra time could not separate the teams in front of 79,347.

MONDAY 16TH MAY 1932

The Owls drew 2-2 against Austrian side Nicholson in a friendly played in Amsterdam. The match referee failed to appear and one of the crowd took the whistle – many of his decisions "left much to be desired".

WEDNESDAY 16TH MAY 1951

The Festival of Britain was held in May 1951 and a series of British v. Foreign friendly games were arranged as part of the British trade celebration, the Owls drawing 0-0 with Danish club Frem.

MONDAY 16TH MAY 2005

On an unforgettable night, the Beatles song Hey Jude became a new theme tune, after a reworking from Owls fans, and more importantly Wednesday won 2-1 at Brentford to seal their place in the play-off final.

MONDAY 17TH MAY 1948

In a friendly on the Isle of Man, 8,000 fans watched Wednesday and United draw 2-2 in the first meeting of the two rivals on neutral territory.

TUESDAY 17TH MAY 1961

A friendly game in Enugh against East Nigeria boiled over in the second half with police running onto the pitch when the teams started to throw punches! Wednesday had scored through Colin Dobson, and a Tom McAnearney penalty, and eventually won 2-1.

MONDAY 17TH MAY 1982

In front of a sparse Hillsborough crowd, a scratch Wednesday side thrashed Doncaster Rovers 9-1 in a Sheffield County Cup tie, 17-year-old striker Tony Simmons netting six times.

SUNDAY 18TH MAY 1952

In a friendly in Geneva, Switzerland the Owls lost 2-1 to Italian side Inter Milan.

SATURDAY 18TH MAY 1963

In the final game of the 1962/63 season, Wednesday lost 3-2 at home to Arsenal – Gerry Young grabbing an equaliser after 88 minutes only for Arsenal to score a minute later to pinch the points.

SUNDAY 19TH MAY 1935

The Owls' friendly against a Copenhagen XI in Denmark was notable for the fact that, as an experiment, two referees were used. A 12,000 crowd turned out to see the FA Cup holders delight the Danish fans by winning 8-2.

THURSDAY 19TH MAY 1966

In a benefit game for former Owl Alan Finney, Wednesday lost 6-5 to Doncaster Rovers in front of 7,027 at Belle Vue.

WEDNESDAY 20TH MAY 1970

On this day Wednesday were in the little Italian town of Savoia where they beat the local side 2-0 on a dusty pitch that was watered by a cart before the game and at half-time! When the home side managed a shot on target the crowd went wild and the referee was so excited that he ran over and kissed the player!

THURSDAY 20TH MAY 1993

Traffic chaos meant many Owls fans missed the kick off to the FA Cup final replay against Arsenal. The teams found themselves deadlocked at 1-1 again after goals from Ian Wright and Chris Waddle but seconds before penalties would have decided the issue an Andy Linighan header somehow slipped through Chris Woods' fingers to break Wednesday hearts.

TUESDAY 21ST MAY 1935

In front of 30,000 in Copenhagen, the touring Owls beat a selected side 6-2 with Jackie Thompson netting a hat-trick.

SATURDAY 21ST MAY 1961

In the final game of their Nigerian tour the Owls failed to win for the first time, sharing four goals with Northern Nigeria in Lagos.

MONDAY 22ND MAY 1967

In a unique swap deal the Springett brothers switched clubs with Ron signing for Queens Park Rangers and younger brother, Peter, moving to Wednesday. On the same day the Owls won 4-1 in a friendly at Wellington Town.

FRIDAY 22ND MAY 1987

In the final game of their tour of Canada, Wednesday drew 0-0 with Calgary Kickers at the Metata Stadium, Alberta.

THURSDAY 23RD MAY 1957

Jimmy Stewart died in Durham. The attacker was twice capped by England during six years at Wednesday (1902-08) and netted 60 goals in 141 games.

SATURDAY 23RD MAY 1970

Wednesday lost 2-0 at Juventus in their final group game in the Anglo-Italian Cup.

TUESDAY 24TH MAY 1960

In their first game behind the 'Iron Curtain', Wednesday lost 1-0 to the Soviet Army team (CSKA Moscow) in front of 50,000 fans in the Central Lenin Stadium, Moscow.

FRIDAY 24TH MAY 1974

With debts spiralling, Wednesday announced increases in season ticket prices for 1974/75, despite having only just escaped relegation. On average, prices rose by around 20% with fans deeply unimpressed!

MONDAY 25TH MAY 1925

Wednesday paid Crystal Palace £500 for their prolific scorer George Whitworth. The centre-forward had netted 50 times for the Eagles in 118 games but never played a first-team game for Wednesday – moving to Hull City at a £200 profit six months later.

MONDAY 25TH MAY 1936

Jack Ashley grabbed a hat-trick and Jackie Robinson a brace, as a Danish Select XI side were beaten 6-0 at 'The Stadium', Copenhagen.

FRIDAY 26TH MAY 1911

In the fourth game of the Owls' first-ever foreign tour, they won 3-2 against a Copenhagen XI.

MONDAY 26TH MAY 1947

Wednesday banished relegation fears, beating Second Division champions-elect Manchester City, 1-0 at Hillsborough. A goal after 17 minutes from Tommy Ward brought relief to the 33,390 crowd as the club, for the second time in three seasons, just avoided the drop into regional football.

FRIDAY 27TH MAY 1966

In the opening game of the club's tour of Far East Asia, Wednesday beat a Hong Kong select side 2-1, watched by 18,000 in the Hong Kong Stadium.

FRIDAY 27TH MAY 1983

After almost six years in charge, manager Jack Charlton resigned from his post. He had stayed a year longer than he intended but had dragged the Owls from the depths of the Third Division to the brink of the top flight.

SATURDAY 28TH MAY 1960

After travelling the huge distance between Moscow and Tiflis (in modern day Georgia) the Owls lost 1-0 to Tbilisi Dynamo.

TUESDAY 28TH MAY 1991

In Ron Atkinson's final act as Owls boss, he sold John Newsome and David Wetherall to Leeds United for a bargain £300,000 fee. The Owls later bought Newsome back for £1.6m!

TUESDAY 29TH MAY 1917

Jack Marshall was born in Bolton on this day. He joined Wednesday as manager in February 1968 and after a spell of illness resigned in March 1969, following a 5-0 home defeat to Arsenal.

SUNDAY 29TH MAY 2005

It was great to be a Wednesday fan on this day as over 40,000 travelled to Cardiff to see their team win a thrilling League One play-off final 4-2 against Hartlepool United. Watched by 59,808, J. P. McGovern, Steve MacLean (pen), Glenn Whelan and Drew Talbot scored for the Owls to earn promotion back to the second level of English football.

THURSDAY 30TH MAY 1935

Wednesday brought their two-week post season European tour to a close with a 4-0 win over Racing Club de France.

SATURDAY 30TH MAY 1985

The Owls met Watford at the Din Daeng Stadium, Bangkok, Thailand in an exhibition match. On a muddy, waterlogged pitch just 2,000 fans saw the game finish 0-0 with Wednesday winning 3-2 in a penalty shoot out.

SATURDAY 31ST MAY 1919

In the final game before the return of national football, Wednesday won 2-1 against Everton in a friendly at Goodison Park, Teddy Glennon netting twice for the Owls in front of a 5,000 crowd.

TUESDAY 31ST MAY 1994

Chris Bart-Williams won his sixth England under-21 cap as an Owl – playing in the 3-0 defeat to France in the Toulon tournament.

SHEFFIELD WEDNESDAY
On This Day

JUNE

WEDNESDAY 1st JUNE 1960

The Owls completed their ambitious tour of the USSR with a 3-2 loss to Locomotiv Moscow in the Lenin Stadium. The Russians led 3-0 after 50 minutes but a late fightback almost earned a draw as Alan Finney scored twice.

WEDNESDAY 1st JUNE 1966

Wednesday and fellow First Division side Fulham met in a friendly played in Hong Kong. Wednesday won 5-2 with David Ford scoring twice.

FRIDAY 2nd JUNE 2000

Local businessman and self-made millionaire, Dave Allen, joined the Owls football and Plc board of directors in a non-executive role.

SATURDAY 2nd JUNE 2007

Wednesday right-back Frank Simek won his second full cap for the USA against China, in San Jose, California.

SUNDAY 3rd JUNE 1934

Wednesday boss Billy Walker acted as referee as his side defeated a Malmo combined team 9-1 in Sweden, on the club's tour of Scandinavia. Inside-forward Harry Burgess led the way with four goals while Ellis Rimmer, Neil Dewar, Ron Starling and Sedley Cooper (2) completed the scoring.

THURSDAY 3rd JUNE 1993

Both Viv Anderson and Danny Wilson left Hillsborough, joining Barnsley as manager and player-coach respectively.

SUNDAY 4th JUNE 1967

Wednesday played their first game in the Hexagonal tournament played at the Aztec Stadium in Mexico City. Local side Toluca were beaten 4-1 with John Ritchie netting twice, watched by a bumper 40,000 crowd.

SUNDAY 4th JUNE 2000

Wednesday's youth team triumphed in the Enschede tournament in Holland. A goal from James Tevendale secured a 1-0 win over Mexican side Cruz Azul in the final, after the Owls had beaten the hosts, a USA under-19 side and Dutch sides Heracles and FC Twente.

THURSDAY 5TH JUNE 1930

Jimmy Trotter was sold to Torquay United for a £500 fee. He ended his playing days at Watford and later worked as a coach at Charlton Athletic.

SUNDAY 5TH JUNE 1966

Wednesday turned on the style as an Asian All Stars side were beaten 5-1 in Kuala Lumpur, Malaysia. A crowd of around 20,000 watched Jim McCalliog (2), Graham Pugh (2) and Peter Eustace score for the Owls and Cheong Chi Doy being almost invited to score by the Owls defence with five minutes remaining!

WEDNESDAY 6TH JUNE 1962

Popular forward Mark Bright was born in Stoke. His goals in the early 1990s made him a huge favourite with Wednesday fans. His extra-time winner against United in the 1993 FA Cup semi-final at Wembley stands out among 70 goals in 170 appearances.

THURSDAY 6TH JUNE 1991

Wednesdayites were stunned when just seven days after being persuaded to stay at Hillsborough, manager Ron Atkinson quit to join Aston Villa.

SATURDAY 6TH JUNE 1992

The Owls' John Harkes equalised for the USA in the 1-1 draw with Italy in Washington DC.

SATURDAY 7TH JUNE 1947

Due to the terrible winter of 1946 the Owls played their final game of the season, at Chesterfield, on the first Saturday in June – the latest a season has ever been completed. The Spireites won 4-2 with full-back George Milburn uniquely scoring a hat-trick of penalty kicks.

WEDNESDAY 7TH JUNE 1989

Ipswich Town forward Dalian Atkinson was signed by his namesake, Ron, for a £450,000 fee. He scored 15 in 45 games in his one season at Wednesday.

FRIDAY 8TH JUNE 1934

Wednesday registered a 6-0 win against a Danish Select XI, in Copenhagen, during the club's post season tour of Scandinavia.

SATURDAY 8TH JUNE 1991

Owls striker David Hirst won his second cap for England during the post season tour Down Under. He entered the fray as a substitute and scored England's second goal, after 50 minutes, in a 2-0 win over New Zealand, in Wellington.

MONDAY 9TH JUNE 1924

Wednesday paid £510 to Raith Rovers for half-back William Collier. The Scot was famously shipwrecked in 1923 when the vessel taking his Raith side on a pre season tour to the Canary Islands ran aground on a sandbank near northern Spain!

SUNDAY 9TH JUNE 1996

Hillsborough Park was crammed full of friendly Danish fans – drinking copious amounts of lager – as their country faced Portugal in the opening game in Group D of the European Championship finals. An entertaining game ended 1-1 in front of a 34,993 Hillsborough crowd.

SUNDAY 10TH JUNE 1962

Wednesday goalkeeper Ron Springett won his 25th cap for England as they lost 3-1 to Brazil in the quarter-finals of the 1962 World Cup, held in Chile. Springett went on to win a total of 33 caps for England – the most decorated England player in the Owls' history.

SUNDAY 10TH JUNE 1990

Owls right-back Roland Nilsson played for Sweden as they lost 2-1 to Brazil in the opening game of their World Cup group in Italy. The Swedish side also contained Klas Ingesson who signed for Wednesday just over four years later.

SUNDAY 11TH JUNE 1967

The Owls were thrashed 5-0 by a Mexican Select XI in front of 45,000 inside the Aztec Stadium.

SATURDAY 11TH JUNE 1994

Northern Ireland lost 3-0 to Mexico in Miami, Florida with Nigel Worthington winning his 50th cap since joining Wednesday; the tally being a club record for international appearances whilst on the Owls' books.

FRIDAY 12TH JUNE 1936

Donald Harry Megson was born in Sale, Cheshire. Although a left winger when he joined the Owls for £50 from non-league Mossley, he would make his name after being moved to left-back by Owls manager Harry Caterrick. He ended his playing days at Bristol Rovers in the early 1970s and in later life worked as a scout – mainly for his son, Gary.

MONDAY 12TH JUNE 2000

Pre-war defender David Wallace Russell died in Birkenhead, aged 86. The Scot cost the Owls £2,000 in 1938 and appeared in 50 first-team games before the Second World War effectively ended his playing days.

SATURDAY 13TH JUNE 1908

Diminutive winger Jack Wilkinson was born in Wath-upon-Dearne. He made his name in local football with Wath Athletic before Bob Brown took him to Hillsborough in October 1925. He helped Wednesday to the Second Division title in his first season and was understudy to Ellis Rimmer as the Owls won consecutive league titles in the late 1920s.

THURSDAY 13TH JUNE 1968

Born in Worksop on this day was Simon Coleman. He joined the Owls on loan in November 1993 and the 6ft central defender joined permanently in January 1994. He made 21 appearances prior to joining Bolton Wanderers for £350,000 in October 1994.

TUESDAY 14TH JUNE 1966

The Owls ended their six-game tour of the Far East in Singapore when Fulham won 4-2, watched by 10,000 fans.

SUNDAY 14TH JUNE 1992

Both Carlton Palmer and Chris Woods were in the England side that drew 0-0 with France, in the finals of the European Championships, held in Sweden.

WEDNESDAY 14TH JUNE 1995

Wednesday officially appointed David Pleat as the club's 17th manager. The Owls were still in dispute with Pleat's former club – Luton Town – and the new man could not officially take up his new duties immediately.

THURSDAY 15TH JUNE 2000

Wednesday winger Niclas Alexandersson played for Sweden in the 0-0 draw against Turkey in Euro 2004. It would be the only point Sweden won as they disappointingly failed to reach the knockout stage.

SUNDAY 15TH JUNE 2008

Jamaican international Deon Burton won his sixth cap while at Wednesday, appearing in a World Cup qualifying game against The Bahamas.

THURSDAY 16TH JUNE 1983

Chris Stringer was born in Grimsby. He came through the youth ranks to make his debut after just 13 seconds of the 2000/01 season. Unfortunately, he suffered a series of injury problems, culminating in his forced retirement after just 12 games, in May 2004.

SUNDAY 16TH JUNE 1996

Hillsborough hosted the Viking hordes again as Denmark faced Croatia. The team from the former Yugoslavia won 3-0 with neutrals in the ground impressed when a sublime chip from Davor Suker soared over the rather embarrassed Manchester United keeper, Peter Schmeichel!

WEDNESDAY 17TH JUNE 1992

Wednesday right-back Roland Nilsson was in the Sweden side that knocked England out of the European Championship finals.

MONDAY 17TH JUNE 1996

Wednesday appointed former Spurs boss Peter Shreeves as new first-team coach. He later spent eight months as Wednesday boss in 2001.

TUESDAY 18TH JUNE 1991

Former England forward Trevor Francis was appointed the new manager at Wednesday, becoming the first player-manager in the club's history. He took over from the man who signed him for Wednesday, Ron Atkinson.

TUESDAY 18TH JUNE 1996

After a brief spell at Hillsborough, Wednesday sold Yugoslavian Darko Kovacevic to Real Sociedad for £2.5m. A sell-on clause saw the fee rise to a club record £4.6m after Kovacevic joined Juventus for £12m in 1999!

MONDAY 19TH JUNE 1972

George Drury died in Hucknall, aged 58. His sale to Arsenal, for £7,000 in March 1938, caused furore among Wednesday fans who accused the club of selling the 'crown jewels' as the side struggled against relegation.

WEDNESDAY 19TH JUNE 1996

The final Euro 96 game held at Hillsborough was easily won 3-0 by Denmark against Turkey.

TUESDAY 20TH JUNE 1911

Born in Barnsley, Joe Cockroft played for both Sheffield clubs and after 97 games for the Owls he became the first player for 59 years to transfer directly between the teams, when he moved in 1948.

TUESDAY 20TH JUNE 1967

Game four of the hexagonal Mexican tournament brought defeat number three as a first-half penalty gave Italian side Bologna a 1-0 win.

THURSDAY 21ST JUNE 1928

James English McConnell died in his native Ireland. He played 50 times for Wednesday and famously introduced a short-lived mascot to Hillsborough when 'Jacko' the live monkey attended an FA Cup tie. Wednesday lost the game but McConnell would forever be referred to as 'Monkey'.

WEDNESDAY 21ST JUNE 2000

After resigning from Bradford City, Paul Jewell became the Owls' new manager, on a three-year contract. Caretaker Peter Shreeves became assistant but reserve boss Chris Waddle resigned after failing to land either role.

FRIDAY 22ND JUNE 1979

The Owls signed Andy McCulloch from Brentford for a £60,000 fee. The no-nonsense attacker scored 49 goals in 149 games for Wednesday before moving to Crystal Palace in the summer of 1983.

THURSDAY 22ND JUNE 1967

Tempers boiled over in the Owls' 1-1 draw against America FC, in the final game in the Mexico City tournament, as both Coco Gomez and Wednesday's Sam Ellis were sent off.

MONDAY 23rd JUNE 1975

Peter Fox signed professional forms, after graduating from the youth ranks. After 52 games for Wednesday he amassed 477 appearances for Stoke City.

SATURDAY 23rd JUNE 2001

Perhaps the only player to have his debut deemed ineligible, Bob Curry died on this day in Halstead, Essex. His sole appearance for Wednesday came at Aston Villa in September 1937 but it later transpired that Wednesday had not registered his transfer correctly!

THURSDAY 24th JUNE 1982

Wednesday captured the signature of vastly experienced Everton defender Mike Lyons for a bargain fee, in hindsight, of £80,000.

SATURDAY 24th JUNE 1995

A scratch side lost 1-0 at Swiss club FC Basel in the Intertoto Cup; former striker John Pearson made a cameo appearance for the club, more than ten years after his last!

SATURDAY 25th JUNE 1932

Ron Starling was signed from Newcastle United for £3,250. Described as the 'man with fluttering feet' he scored 30 times for Wednesday in 193 games.

MONDAY 25th JUNE 2007

The Hillsborough pitch was submerged under 6ft of water in the worst-ever flooding to hit Sheffield. After the river Don burst its banks the ground was overwhelmed by water, causing over £1m of damage, with the South Stand, including the dressing rooms, the club shop and tickets office all badly hit.

FRIDAY 26th JUNE 1914

Derwick Ormond Goodfellow was born in the Northumberland village of Shilbottle. The goalie signed in May 1936 from Gateshead and made a total of 77 appearances, either side of the war.

SATURDAY 26th JUNE 1926

At the tender age of just 37, Teddy Glennon died in Ashby de la Zouch, Leicestershire. The strong inside-forward has been a regular at Hillsborough for almost a decade and later played first-class cricket for Leicestershire.

TUESDAY 27TH JUNE 1950

Wednesday released their annual accounts, showing a profit of £10,591 for the 1949/50 promotion season. Total turnover was a healthy £80,727 in a season where the club's average crowd was 40,682.

TUESDAY 27TH JUNE 2000

Assistant manager Frank Barlow left the club after the arrival of Paul Jewell as manager. The former Chesterfield manager initially joined the Owls as youth boss in 1988 and later moved into a senior coaching role under Ron Atkinson and Trevor Francis.

FRIDAY 28TH JUNE 1929

Inside-forward Harold Hill moved to Midland League Scarborough after 40 goals in 99 games for Wednesday.

FRIDAY 28TH JUNE 1974

Fred Lester died in Chatham, Kent. He had been understudy to England full-back Ted Catlin during seven years at Wednesday from 1937 to 1944.

THURSDAY 29TH JUNE 1899

The Wednesday signed centre-forward Harry Millar for the princely sum of £100. He debuted in the first game at Owlerton and hit 14 goals in 28 league games as Wednesday won the Second Division championship in 1900.

SATURDAY 29TH JUNE 1929

Wednesday signed Welsh international Tommy Jones from Tranmere Rovers for £1,500. The winger would add two caps for his country while at Hillsborough but in the main was understudy to Mark Hooper.

FRIDAY 30TH JUNE 2000

Spanish lollipop maker Chupa Chups was announced as the club's new shirt sponsor, signing a two-year £1m deal.

MONDAY 30TH JUNE 2008

Lee Bullen, Burton O'Brien, Rob Burch and Ronnie Wallwork were all released at the end of their contracts. For Bullen it marked the end of four years at Wednesday where he had amassed 148 appearances and captained the club to Cardiff glory in 2005 – the highlight of his professional career.

SHEFFIELD WEDNESDAY
On This Day

JULY

FRIDAY 1st JULY 1994

After just over five years at Hillsborough, former record signing Carlton Palmer was sold to Premiership rivals Leeds United for £2.75m. He would return to Wednesday for two further spells, eventually totalling 286 appearances, scoring 18 goals.

TUESDAY 1st JULY 2003

On a busy day for manager Chris Turner, he signed three players on Bosman free transfers; Hartlepool United duo Paul Smith and Graeme Lee plus Swedish goalkeeper Ola Tidman.

SATURDAY 2nd JULY 1994

Wednesday inside-forward Arnold Lowes passed away in Sheffield. He made 44 appearances for the Owls – either side of the Second World War – and netted ten goals.

SATURDAY 2nd JULY 2005

Midfielder Tommy Miller moved back to his native north-east, signing for Sunderland from Ipswich Town on this day. After a second spell at Portman Road he joined the Owls on July 1st 2009, on a two-year contract.

THURSDAY 3rd JULY 1975

Born in Cowes, Isle of Wight, Lee Bradbury spent two loan periods at Hillsborough. His first was cut short through a shoulder injury in January 2003 while he spent a further six weeks on the Owls' books later in the 2002/03 campaign – scoring three times in a total of 11 games.

WEDNESDAY 3rd JULY 2002

The Owls won the chase to sign free agent Lloyd Owusu, who had left Brentford after scoring 20 goals as the London club reached the Second Division play off final. He would spend a relatively unproductive time in Wednesday colours, scoring only nine times in 60 games.

FRIDAY 4th JULY 1947

Scottish midfielder Malcolm Darling was born in Arbroath. His career at Hillsborough lasted only 27 days – in September 1977 – and he failed to impress the Wednesday faithful in three appearances as the club struggled desperately at the wrong end of the Third Division.

MONDAY 4TH JULY 1994

The Republic of Ireland exited the USA 1994 World Cup, losing 2-0 to Holland with the Owls' John Sheridan on the losing side.

TUESDAY 5TH JULY 1955

The Owls paid Notts County an initial £6,800 for the transfer of winger Albert Broadbent but the deal also included a rather strange 'add on' clause that guaranteed County £50 for every goal their former player netted in 1955/56. He scored 12 so the Magpies received an extra £600!

FRIDAY 5TH JULY 1985

In the Leeds district of Ossett, Richard Wood was born. He joined the Owls before reaching his teenage years and signed professional in March 2003, making his debut in April 2003. He passed the 150-game mark during the 2008/09 season and now captains the club.

WEDNESDAY 6TH JULY 1977

Con Blatsis was born in Melbourne, Australia. The 6ft 3ins. defender appeared in eight games for the Owls, on loan from Derby County, between December 2001 and February 2002. He returned home after a disastrous spell in Turkish football and now plays for South Melbourne in the Victoria Premier League.

MONDAY 6TH JULY 1998

Former player Danny Wilson returned to Hillsborough as manager, controversially leaving newly relegated neighbours Barnsley to take over at the Owls. In 1997 he had led the Tykes into the Premiership for the first time in their history.

MONDAY 7TH JULY 1924

Born on this day in Glasgow, Matt 'Laurie' MacKenzie arrived at Wednesday from Clydebank for a £25 fee in March 1946. He only made six appearances for the club in three years at Hillsborough and is perhaps best remembered for his Middlewood Road bakery shop, *Dora Websters*, which he ran with his wife for several decades. The business was sold for £175,000 in June 2008 after no member of the family wanted to continue to bake bread, pastries and buns.

SATURDAY 8TH JULY 1995

At their temporary home of Millmoor, a 5,592 crowd watched the Owls beat Polish side Gornik Zabrze 3-2 in the second game in the Intertoto Cup competition.

TUESDAY 8TH JULY 2003

Making his first appearance in an Owls shirt, Graeme Lee netted a hat-trick of headers as Dutch club VV Dovo were beaten 5-0 in a pre season friendly.

THURSDAY 8TH JULY 2004

Steve MacLean signed from Glasgow Rangers for a £125,000 fee. He had spent the previous season on loan at Scunthorpe United, scoring 28 times.

MONDAY 9TH JULY 1973

Over two years after being sacked as Owls boss, Danny Williams agreed to take a 'golden handshake' of £10,000 from Wednesday to finally settle the protracted dispute between the two parties.

TUESDAY 9TH JULY 1935

After 47 appearances for Wednesday in almost five years at the club, goalkeeper Jack Breedon moved to Manchester United for a £350 fee.

WEDNESDAY 10TH JULY 1991

The Owls equalled their transfer record by paying Oldham Athletic £750,000 for defender Paul Warhurst. Wednesday almost quadrupled their money when he moved to Blackburn Rovers in 1993.

SATURDAY 10TH JULY 1999

The Owls completed the signing of Belgium international striker Gilles De Bilde on a lucrative contract, paying PSV Eindhoven £2.8m. Within two years he was back home with the Owls failing to recoup any of the fee!

THURSDAY 11TH JULY 1929

Brilliant 19th century winger Billy Mosforth passed away in Sheffield, aged 71. Nicknamed the 'Little Wonder' he appeared in the club's first FA Cup tie, scored six times in 25 FA Cup games for the Owls and was capped for England at the age of just 19. Standing only 5ft 3ins. tall he is regarded as the smallest player ever to represent Wednesday.

MONDAY 11TH JULY 2005

In a bizarre move, Wednesday re-signed goalkeeper Chris Adamson just 11 days after he had been released! He stayed for another two seasons but was only ever number two and appeared in 12 games before leaving in 2007.

TUESDAY 12TH JULY 1966

Hillsborough hosted its first World Cup match as 36,000 watched West Germany beat Switzerland 5-0 – Franz Beckenbauer scoring twice.

TUESDAY 12TH JULY 2005

The Owls sent their first team to Dronfield to face Sheffield Football Club in a pre-season game. Two goals apiece from Chris Brunt, Steve MacLean and Lee Peacock helped Wednesday win 7-1.

MONDAY 13TH JULY 1925

Former England international, George Wilson, made the rather strange move from Wednesday to Division Three (North) strugglers Nelson. The Lancashire minnows paid the Owls a record fee of £2,350 with the promise of a public house in Nelson the main reason for the move.

WEDNESDAY 13TH JULY 1983

New manager Howard Wilkinson completed his backroom staff when recruiting physio Alan Smith from Blackpool. He would later become physio to the full England side and returned to Wednesday in February 2009 as the club's medical consultant.

TUESDAY 13TH JULY 2004

Wednesday beat Preston North End 3-2 in the Copa de Ibiza tournament. Goals from Chris Marsden, Steve MacLean and Adam Proudlock at the San Antonio Stadium put Wednesday into the final, to the delight of a large Owls support.

SUNDAY 14TH JULY 1901

Diminutive winger – 5ft 5ins. – Mark Hooper was born in Darlington. Wednesday paid his hometown club £1,950 for his services in January 1927 and Hooper became a darling of the Owls fans, netting 135 times in 423 competitive games. He also set a club record of 189 consecutive appearances – a mark that would stand for over 50 years.

WEDNESDAY 14TH JULY 1993

Wednesday paid a club record fee of £2.75m for the signature of Des Walker from Sampdoria. Despite the large fee he proved great value, leading from the back for eight years.

SATURDAY 15TH JULY 1995

A 1-1 draw in Germany, against Karlsruher SC, meant the Owls could not progress to the next stage of the Intertoto Cup. A late equaliser from Mark Bright had raised hopes amongst the Owls fans in the 13,000 crowd.

THURSDAY 15TH JULY 2004

The final of the Copa de Ibiza, against Watford, went to penalties after the sides drew 1-1 after 90 minutes in the San Antonio Stadium. The Hornets won the penalty competition.

SATURDAY 15TH JULY 2006

In one of the strangest games in the Owls' long history, over three hours were needed to finish the friendly in North Carolina against Wilmington Hammerheads. With the game tied at 0-0 after 37 minutes a violent electrical storm hit the area, causing all the players, officials and fans (including your author!) to take cover under the stands. After a delay of 75 minutes the game re-started with just the second half being played, much to the surprise of the small travelling band of Wednesday fans in the ground! A late goal from Kenny Lunt tied the game at 1-1.

SATURDAY 16TH JULY 1966

Former Owls captain Jimmy Seed passed away in Farnborough at the age of 71. His impact on the Owls side of the late 1920s was truly inspirational as they were transformed from certain relegation candidates to league champions inside twelve months.

TUESDAY 16TH JULY 2002

Wednesday opened their tour of Scandinavia on a scorching hot day, with a 1-1 draw against FC Copenhagen, played in the little village of Helsingor. Wednesday went ahead through Phil O'Donnell only for the host club to level with just two minutes remaining.

WEDNESDAY 17TH JULY 1946

The club announced season ticket prices for the 1946/47 season with non-members being able to reserve a seat for £5, an enclosure ticket for £2, 10 shillings and a ground ticket for £1, 10 shillings. Shareholders could get a seat for just £3 in the best stand!

FRIDAY 17TH JULY 1992

Wednesday completed the signing of England international Chris Waddle from French side Marseille. The £1m fee proved a bargain as Waddle became a huge success, netting 15 goals in 157 games in blue and white, and became the only Wednesday player to win the prestigious Football Writers' award.

MONDAY 18TH JULY 1955

After two goals in 107 games for Wednesday, former England international Ron Staniforth moved to league side Barrow. He would later coach back at Hillsborough in the 1970s.

SATURDAY 18TH JULY 1987

New signing David Armstrong made his Owls debut as a sub in a 0-0 pre season draw in Germany, against DSC Arminia Bielefeld. The 45 minutes proved to be the former England international's only appearance in an Owls shirt as, bizarrely, his newly signed contract was almost immediately torn up so he could move to AFC Bournemouth instead.

MONDAY 19TH JULY 1993

The Owls went goal crazy in a pre-season friendly at Cornish side Bodmin Town, winning 9-2 with Paul Warhurst netting a hat-trick and Mark Bright scoring twice.

SATURDAY 19TH JULY 2003

A hat-trick from Shefki Kuqi saw the Owls recover from an early goal to beat Macclesfield Town 3-1 in a Moss Road friendly.

THURSDAY 20TH JULY 1905

Born in Ashington, George Alfred Johnson made only one appearance for the Owls, scoring in a 4-0 win, in three years at Hillsborough. He acted as reserve to Wednesday greats Jack Allen and Jack Ball so therefore spent 99% of his playing time in the reserves.

WEDNESDAY 20TH JULY 1994

Wednesday beat Shimizu S-Pulse 4-3, watched by a huge 44,037 crowd, inside the Tokyo Dome. Grass had been laid especially inside the dome for the game with Ian Taylor hitting an 83rd-minute winner.

WEDNESDAY 21ST JULY 1965

Wednesday caused controversy when announcing that they would be dispensing with their traditional striped jerseys – introducing a new 'modern' all blue shirt with white arms.

SUNDAY 21ST JULY 1991

Hillsborough hosted the semi-finals of the football section of the World Student Games. The entertaining South Koreans beat Uruguay 4-1 while Great Britain lost 1-0 to the Netherlands.

FRIDAY 22ND JULY 1960

Popular 1980s forward Gary Bannister was born in Warrington, Lancashire. He became the first Wednesday player for almost fifty years to score over twenty goals in three consecutive seasons and proved one of Jack Charlton's best ever signings.

SUNDAY 22ND JULY 1984

In a charity game, the Owls won 25-1 against a side drawn from the Royal Oak Hotel in Keswick. Thirteen Wednesday men found the net – including manager Howard Wilkinson and his assistant Peter Eustace – while the home side's consolation goal was scored when the Owls' goalie had his hand tied to the post by a group of cheerleaders!

SATURDAY 23RD JULY 1966

The Owls started their pre-season in the unlikely setting of Varna in Bulgaria, drawing 2-2 against Spartak Varna. Meanwhile back in Sheffield a Hillsborough crowd of 40,007 saw West Germany thrash Uruguay 4-0 to reach the semi-final of the World Cup.

SATURDAY 23RD JULY 1973

In the VIF Cup tournament in Sweden, the Owls won 4-2 against IFK Eskilstuna although John Holsgrove was sent off with two minutes remaining.

WEDNESDAY 24TH JULY 2002

With former Rangers player Scott Wilson handed a trial game at centre-half, Wednesday won 2-0 at Partick Thistle in Glasgow. Gerald Sibon and Leon Knight netted for Wednesday at the Firhill Stadium.

SUNDAY 24TH JULY 2005

The Owls lost 2-1 to Dundee United in the final of the City of Discovery Cup, a tournament played at the grounds of both Dundee clubs. Wednesday reached the Dens Park final by beating Wolves 24 hours previously.

TUESDAY 25TH JULY 1899

Sid Binks was born at Whitworth, near Bishop Auckland. After winning England amateur caps while at Bishop Auckland he scored three hat-tricks for Wednesday after turning professional in May 1922. He scored 33 goals in 83 games and later in life ran a bakery in Sheffield.

THURSDAY 25TH JULY 1991

Walter Rickett died, aged 74, in Kettering. After eight years at Sheffield United he transferred to Wednesday in October 1949, making 97 appearances before completing a South Yorkshire triple by joining Rotherham United.

SUNDAY 26TH JULY 1987

The Owls wound up their pre season tour of Germany by losing 1-0 to Shalke 04, in front of 7,000 fans.

FRIDAY 26TH JULY 1996

Wednesday played for the final time at Brighton & Hove Albion's Goldstone Ground, winning 7-1 in a benefit match for popular defender Steve Foster – a hat-trick from David Hirst contributing to the comprehensive win.

THURSDAY 27TH JULY 1939

Professional tennis came to Hillsborough with 10,000 fans in attendance to see an event dubbed as 'Three Hours of Wimbledon'.

THURSDAY 27TH JULY 1989

The Owls started pre season with a 5-0 win at Witney Town with £300,000 signing Craig Shakespeare amongst the scorers. The new man played only 21 games before leaving for West Bromwich Albion.

WEDNESDAY 28TH JULY 1948

Arguably the most colourful character in the Owls' history, Fred Spiksley, collapsed and died on Ladies Day at Goodwood Races. Legend states that Fred – a keen follower of the 'Sport of Kings' – backed the 100-8 winner of the 3.10 race but did not live to collect his winnings.

FRIDAY 28TH JULY 2006

Out of favour attacker David Graham joined Bradford City on loan until the New Year while Owls youngster Rory McArdle won his first under-20 cap for Northern Ireland.

TUESDAY 29TH JULY 1930

The Owls paid Manchester United £1,300 for the services of centre-forward Jack Ball.

SATURDAY 29TH JULY 2000

The Owls had Brazilian trialist Nei in goal for a pre-season friendly at Scunthorpe United. Wednesday led 2-0 but lost 3-2 to a last-minute goal from the home side. More irritating for Owls fans on the day was a plague of small black flies that seemed to be everywhere!

WEDNESDAY 30TH JULY 1969

Wednesday hosted Aberdeen in a pre-season game at Hillsborough, winning 2-1 thanks to goals from John Fantham and David Ford.

WEDNESDAY 30TH JULY 1986

In the inaugural game for the Finlux Cup, the Owls lost 3-2 at HJK Helsinki in the first of three pre-season games played in Scandinavia.

SATURDAY 31ST JULY 1993

In front of almost 25,000 at Celtic Park, the Owls drew 1-1 with Glasgow Celtic. A Frank McAvennie penalty put the home side ahead before Paul Warhurst equalised to share the spoils.

SUNDAY 31ST JULY 2005

The Owls suffered a huge blow in their final pre-season game, against Manchester City at Hillsborough, as 2004/05 top scorer Steve MacLean broke his tibia in the 1-1 draw.

SHEFFIELD WEDNESDAY
On This Day

AUGUST

SATURDAY 1st AUGUST 1908

Wednesday fans were shocked when outstanding attacker James Stewart was sold to First Division rivals Newcastle United for £1,000.

WEDNESDAY 1st AUGUST 1990

After just one season in a Wednesday shirt, Dalian Atkinson was sold to Spanish side Real Sociedad for a £1.7m fee – the first time the club had received over £1m for a player.

FRIDAY 1st AUGUST 1997

The Owls beat TOP Oss 3-1, in the small Dutch town of Oss. The initials of Wednesday's opponents bizarrely translated as "until our pleasure".

TUESDAY 2nd AUGUST 1927

One of the greatest signings ever made by Wednesday was on this day when Spurs allowed Jimmy Seed to transfer north in part exchange for Arthur Lowdell. He later inspired Wednesday to an astonishing escape from the drop in 1928 (sending Spurs down instead) and then led them to consecutive league titles, scoring 38 times in 146 games.

SATURDAY 2nd AUGUST 1991

USA international John Harkes played for his club side as the Owls lost 2-0 to the US National side in Philadelphia. The friendly game was played in searing heat on Astroturf and attracted 44,261 to the Veterans Stadium.

FRIDAY 2nd AUGUST 1996

The Owls went goal crazy in their first game of a six-game pre season tour of Holland, thrashing minnows SV Gouda 12-0 – both Andy Booth and Guy Whittingham scoring hat-tricks.

SATURDAY 3rd AUGUST 1929

The club officially changed their name from The Wednesday FC to Sheffield Wednesday FC.

MONDAY 3rd AUGUST 1998

Uniquely, the Owls played two 'first-team' games on the same day; the stronger side lost 2-1 at Walsall while a mixed side lost 1-0 to Shrewsbury Town in the Shropshire Cup Final – the Owls were inexplicably invited as guests.

TUESDAY 4TH AUGUST 1970

The Owls crashed 5-0 in a pre-season friendly at First Division Huddersfield Town. All the goals came in the second half against a side that had taken Wednesday's place in the top flight.

SATURDAY 4TH AUGUST 2001

Finalists in the 2000 Uefa Cup, Deportivo Alaves, were beaten 1-0 in a pre-season friendly at Hillsborough. A goal from new signing Paul McLaren was enough to beat the Spaniards.

SATURDAY 5TH AUGUST 1987

The Owls met the Blades at Bramall Lane in a fundraising game for the World Student Games. Goals from Gary Megson, Mark Chamberlain and Mel Sterland resulted in a 3-0 win for Wednesday.

WEDNESDAY 5TH AUGUST 1992

In preparation for their Uefa Cup campaign, the Owls travelled to Athens to play AEK. It was a sobering evening for Wednesday as the hosts recorded a 4-0 win with a penalty and Viv Anderson's own goal contributing to the score.

FRIDAY 6TH AUGUST 1926

The club convened at the Royal Victoria Hotel in Sheffield to celebrate winning the Second Division title and 60th anniversary. Toasts included 'The King', 'The Wednesday Football Club' and 'Visitors and press'.

SATURDAY 6TH AUGUST 2005

Wednesday started the opening game of the season, at Stoke City, with four new signings in their side. Frank Simek, John Hills, Chris Eagles and Leon Best were the quartet with second-half substitute Richie Partridge taking the debuts to five as Wednesday held City to a 0-0 draw, in a game where home player Gerry Taggart was sent off and Kevin Harper blazed a 75th-minute penalty over the bar.

SATURDAY 7TH AUGUST 1976

Two goals apiece from Roger Wylde and Peter Feely took the Owls to a 5-2 success at Cambridge United, meaning Wednesday were the inaugural winners of the Shipp Cup, after winning all three games.

SATURDAY 7TH AUGUST 2004

In front of an expectant 24,138 Hillsborough crowd, Colchester United spoiled the opening day, scoring three in the last five minutes to win 3-0.

FRIDAY 8TH AUGUST 1919

Wednesday appointed William Barr as the club's new trainer. The former Scottish professional player had previously worked at Third Lanark and Raith Rovers but lasted only one season at Hillsborough – leaving after the club were relegated in May 1920.

MONDAY 8TH AUGUST 1966

Hillsborough staged its first ever pre-season friendly, as a Bulgarian Select XI were beaten 2-1 in front of 19,441 fans.

FRIDAY 8TH AUGUST 1997

Italian winger Paolo Di Canio arrived from Celtic for a club record £4.5m. Winger Regi Blinker went to Glasgow in part exchange with Wednesday paying the £3m balance for the fiery and highly talented Roman.

MONDAY 9TH AUGUST 1971

United scored after just 55 seconds at Bramall Lane in a pre-season friendly but Wednesday fought back to draw the game 2-2, thanks to goals in the last fifteen minutes from Steve Downes and Mick Prendergast.

MONDAY 9TH AUGUST 1993

An 82nd-minute strike from David Hirst gave the Owls a 1-0 win at Bramall Lane in a testimonial match for Sheffield football hero Derek Dooley.

SATURDAY 9TH AUGUST 2003

On a scorching hot day in Wiltshire, 3,382 Wednesday fans made the trip to Swindon Town for the opening game of the new season. The Owls went 3-0 up after just 24 minutes but needed a rearguard action to secure a 3-2 Second Division win.

SATURDAY 10TH AUGUST 2002

Only one new face was in the side, Jon Beswetherick, for the opening game of the new season at home to Stoke City. A 26,746 crowd saw a fairly entertaining 0-0 draw.

TUESDAY 10TH AUGUST 2004

Wednesday enjoyed their day at the seaside, winning 2-1 at Blackpool in a League One game, thanks to goals from Lee Bullen and young midfielder Lewis McMahon.

MONDAY 11TH AUGUST 1986

Wednesday completed the signing of Barnsley's teenage striker, David Hirst. The clubs agreed a £200,000 fee although this figure eventually rose to £300,000 after Hirst earned international honours.

WEDNESDAY 11TH AUGUST 1999

Signs of a season of struggle were evident at Old Trafford as Wednesday were comprehensively beaten 4-0 with Cole, Scholes, Yorke and Solskjaer scoring for Manchester United.

SUNDAY 12TH AUGUST 1962

The Owls visited Amsterdam for the second time in two years but this time fell to a 3-1 defeat against Ajax at the De Meer Stadium – Colin Dobson had put Wednesday ahead after five minutes.

SATURDAY 12TH AUGUST 1972

Young striker Roger Wylde netted a double hat-trick as the reserves won 7-0 at Manchester City, in the first Central League game of the new season.

SATURDAY 12TH AUGUST 1978

Ray Blackhall and Peter Shirtliff made their debuts as an own goal gifted the Owls a 1-0 first-leg win at Doncaster Rovers in a League Cup-tie.

SATURDAY 12TH AUGUST 1989

In a friendly to celebrate the 100th birthday of Sheffield United, the two city teams drew 0-0 at Bramall Lane. However, the game proved costly for Wednesday, as key man Carlton Palmer was controversially sent off by referee Keith Hackett, leaving the midfielder suspended for the start of the season.

SUNDAY 12TH AUGUST 2001

Hillsborough played host to the first live game televised by satellite channel ITV Digital. With a bizarre kick-off time of 6.15pm, the Owls lost 2-0 in front of 21,766 fans.

TUESDAY 13th AUGUST 1872

Robert Ferrier was born in Dumbarton, Scotland. One of the Owls' greatest Scottish imports of the Victorian age, Ferrier started his playing career in his homeland with a club that boasted, for some obscure reason, a French name 'L'Homme qui rit' – roughly translated to 'the man who laugh'.

SUNDAY 13th AUGUST 1961

In the club's first ever pre-season friendly, Wednesday won 2-1 against Ajax in Amsterdam with Bobby Craig and John Fantham finding the net.

SATURDAY 13th AUGUST 2000

The Owls set a somewhat unwanted British record when goalkeeper Kevin Pressman was red carded after just 13 seconds of the opening game of the 2000/01 campaign. His replacement, debutant Chris Stringer, performed heroics as a second-half equaliser from Andy Booth secured a battling 1-1 draw at Wolves.

SATURDAY 14th AUGUST 1971

Wednesday made a bad start to the new season by losing 3-0 at Queens Park Rangers – Rodney Marsh (2) and Gerry Francis netting for Rangers. The Owls had John Holsgrove making his debut while 70th-minute sub Kevin Johnson recorded his only first team appearance for Wednesday. The midfielder moved to Southend United in 1972 while his son married the daughter of Wednesday legend Alan Finney.

WEDNESDAY 14th AUGUST 1991

The £1.2m arrival of England goalkeeper Chris Woods, from Glasgow Rangers, marked the first time the Owls had paid a seven-figure sum for a player. Wednesday bought Woods despite having Kevin Pressman, Chris Turner and Marlon Beresford on their books!

SATURDAY 14th AUGUST 1993

With big-money signing Des Walker and fellow new boy Andy Pearce in the Owls' ranks for the first time any hopes of a winning start to the season were dashed at Anfield as Carlton Palmer was red carded after just 12 minutes and Nigel Clough scored twice in front of a 44,004 crowd.

KEVIN PRESSMAN, 478 APPEARANCES BETWEEN 1987 AND 2004

SATURDAY 15TH AUGUST 1970

In their first match out of the top flight for 11 years, the Owls beat Charlton Athletic 1-0 at Hillsborough. A goal from Steve Downes after 75 minutes sealed the two points in front of a 17,152 crowd.

SATURDAY 15TH AUGUST 1992

The Owls drew 1-1 at Everton on the first day of the new season, Nigel Pearson putting Wednesday ahead in the first half. £1m signing Chris Waddle made his competitive debut but was forced off injured after just 39 minutes, with strained knee ligaments.

SATURDAY 15TH AUGUST 1998

Wednesday gave debuts to Wim Jonk and Juan Cobian on the opening day of the new Premiership season. Ian Wright scored the only goal of the game for West Ham United in Danny Wilson's first game in charge of the Owls.

SATURDAY 16TH AUGUST 1975

Wednesday played their first-ever game in the third tier of English football, losing 2-1 at Southend United after Mick Prendergast had given them the lead after 41 minutes.

SATURDAY 16TH AUGUST 1969

After losing their first two games of the new season, Wednesday slumped to last place after losing 3-2 to Wolves in their first home game. The match also saw Derek Dougan and Peter Eustace sent off for fighting.

SATURDAY 16TH AUGUST 1980

In their first game back in the Second Division for five years, Wednesday beat Newcastle United 2-0 at Hillsborough. Second-half goals from Andy McCulloch and Kevin Taylor earned the win in front of a 26,164 crowd.

SATURDAY 17TH AUGUST 1991

The temperature was hot, on and off the pitch, as Ron Atkinson made a swift return to Hillsborough, with Aston Villa, for the opening game of the 1991/92 season. Strikes from David Hirst and Danny Wilson put Wednesday 2-0 ahead after 36 minutes but 'Big Ron' had the last laugh as 36,749 saw Villa win 3-2.

SATURDAY 17TH AUGUST 1996

Wednesday made a fine start to the season as teenager Ritchie Humphreys crashed home a superb goal as Aston Villa were beaten 2-1 at Hillsborough.

FRIDAY 18TH AUGUST 1893

At the Maunchie Hotel in Sheffield, The Wednesday FC was turned into a limited company with 50 shares issued at £5 each.

SATURDAY 18TH AUGUST 1984

Wednesday drew 1-1 at Notts County, in a testimonial match for Ray O'Brien. Only 1,507 attended the game with Gary Shelton scoring a second-half equaliser for Howard Wilkinson's side.

SATURDAY 19TH AUGUST 1967

The Owls controversially lost 3-2 at West Ham United on the opening day of the season with Hammers' England World Cup winner Martin Peters later admitting he had punched his side's second goal into the net!

SUNDAY 19TH AUGUST 2001

Young reserve team regular Tom Staniforth died suddenly, aged just 19, after a night out in his hometown of York.

SATURDAY 20TH AUGUST 1938

To celebrate the Jubilee of the Football League, a series of friendly games were arranged with Wednesday meeting the Blades at Hillsborough. A Doug Hunt hat-trick and goal from Dai Lewis sealed a 4-1 win for Wednesday.

SATURDAY 20TH AUGUST 1949

Wednesday were struck by an injury jinx on the opening day of the new season as Dennis Woodhead broke his leg in the first team's 3-1 win against Leicester City, while goalkeeper Albert Morton fractured his leg 48 hours later in a reserve game at Hillsborough.

SATURDAY 20TH AUGUST 1955

Wednesday made a superb start to their Second Division campaign by beating Plymouth Argyle 5-2 at Hillsborough. The Owls gave debuts to Roy Shiner, Albert Broadbent, Don Gibson and Ron Staniforth although it was 'old boys' Jackie Sewell (3) and Albert Quxiall (2) who clinched the points.

SATURDAY 20TH AUGUST 1994

The nation's eyes were on Hillsborough to see new Spurs signing Jurgen Klinsmann make his debut. The Owls gave debuts to four players themselves – Peter Atherton, Ian Nolan, Dan Petrescu and Ian Taylor – but Klinsmann proved the match winner, scoring Tottenham's final goal in a 4-3 classic.

SATURDAY 21ST AUGUST 1926

The seminal book on the club's early years *The Romance of The Wednesday* was launched on this day.

SATURDAY 21ST AUGUST 1950

Newly promoted Wednesday beat champions Portsmouth in the first home game of the season. A 46,740 crowd saw Hugh McJarrow equalise the scores after 83 minutes and Dennis Woodhead fire home a last-minute winner.

SATURDAY 22ND AUGUST 1936

The club held its public practice match at Hillsborough – a crowd of 4,812 watching the Stripes (first team) beat the Whites (reserves) 2-1 in a game of just 30 minutes each way.

SATURDAY 22ND AUGUST 1992

In a Premiership clash at Hillsborough, Wednesday grabbed a late equaliser through Danny Wilson to draw 3-3 with Chelsea.

SATURDAY 23RD AUGUST 1924

Born on this day in Sheffield, inside-forward Redfern Froggatt played all of his senior football with the Owls, amassing 458 games and helping Wednesday to four promotions after signing during the Second World War.

WEDNESDAY 23RD AUGUST 1961

FA chairman, Sir Stanley Rous, opened Hillsborough's new 'state of the art' Cantilever North Stand prior to the 4-2 win over Bolton Wanderers.

SATURDAY 23RD AUGUST 1986

Wednesday kicked off their First Division campaign with a 1-1 draw against Charlton Athletic, at their temporary Selhurst Park home. A goal from Gary Shelton earned Wednesday a point in a game where teenage forward David Hirst made his debut as a 76th-minute substitute.

SATURDAY 23rd AUGUST 1997

Paolo Di Canio showed a lot of cheek in the 1-1 Premiership draw at Wimbledon, pulling his shorts down to moon the crowd after deflecting the equaliser into the net off his behind! Unfortunately, the FA did not see the funny side and the Italian was subsequently fined £1,000.

WEDNESDAY 23rd AUGUST 2006

Youngsters Matt Bowman and David McClements both made their only senior appearances for Wednesday as Wrexham gained a shock 4-1 League Cup win at Hillsborough. Barnsley-born Bowman was aged just 16 years, 205 days when he appeared from the subs bench, beating the previous record holder, Mark Platts, by 58 days to become the youngest outfield player to play for the club.

MONDAY 24th AUGUST 1903

To celebrate the winning of the First Division championship for the first time, Wednesday held a celebration banquet at the Masonic Hall in Sheffield. The night also paid tribute to the reserve team who won the Midland League, Sheffield Challenge Cup and Wharncliffe Charity Cup. Mr. Callum on the piano accompanied the night's entertainment including tenor Mr. Burrows and humorist Mr. Harry Heath.

SATURDAY 24th AUGUST 1985

A double from Brian Marwood took the Owls to a 3-1 Maine Road win against Manchester City. The victory left Wednesday in second place in the early league tables with seven points from nine. The game also saw Tony Gregory make his debut – he would appear in 21 games for Wednesday and after ending his playing days, qualified as a chiropodist.

SATURDAY 25th AUGUST 1928

In a terrific opening-day game, 23,634 were inside Hillsborough to see Wednesday come from behind twice, through Mark Hooper and Billy Marsden, to level matters at 2-2 against Arsenal. It was then left to Hooper to hit a 68th-minute winner against a Gunners side that ran out onto the pitch wearing shirts with black numbers on a white square – becoming the first team to wear numbered shirts in an English league fixture.

SATURDAY 25TH AUGUST 1945

On the opening day of the new Football League (North) competition, Wednesday beat Sunderland 6-3 at Hillsborough with both Jackie Robinson and Alf Rogers scoring hat-tricks. The former was a darling of the Owls fans and is considered by many to be the greatest player in the club's history – if Robinson's wartime statistics are taken into account the inside-forward scored 129 goals in 229 games for Wednesday although only 119 (39 goals) came in peacetime soccer. The game also marked the debut of Eric Taylor as full-time Wednesday manager following his appointment in June 1945.

SATURDAY 25TH AUGUST 1984

Wednesday made a great start to life back in the top division, as visitors Nottingham Forest were beaten 3-1. A Mel Sterland penalty had put the Owls in front and after Forest had levelled, an outstanding solo goal from Imre Varadi put Wednesday back ahead before John Pearson wrapped up the points in front of 31,925.

MONDAY 25TH AUGUST 1986

The home game with Everton saw the new covered Kop used for the very first time. The new structure lifted the standing capacity at the Penistone Road end of the ground to 22,000 – the biggest in Europe – and 33,007 (including over 17,500 on the Kop) were inside Hillsborough as sub David Hirst netted his first goal for the club in a 2-2 draw.

WEDNESDAY 26TH AUGUST 1953

Wednesday travelled to Preston as early league leaders but that good start ended spectacularly, as the Owls were beaten 6-0. The result did not tell the whole story, however, as with the score at 1-0 Wednesday lost goalkeeper Dave McIntosh with a broken arm. Full-back Norman Curtis took over in goal and amazingly the stand-in saved penalties from Tom Finney and then Jimmy Baxter.

SATURDAY 26TH AUGUST 1961

A hat-trick from John Fantham, and further goals from Keith Ellis and Alan Finney, took Wednesday to a resounding 5-1 First Division win over Birmingham City at Hillsborough.

MONDAY 27TH AUGUST 1923

Billy Felton and Rees Williams missed the train for the trip to Port Vale. Travelling reserve Charlie Petrie filled one place but the strange situation led to the club's trainer – Jerry Jackson – playing on the right wing. Although his precise age is not known it's believed he could have been as old as fifty, easily making Jackson the oldest player to have appeared in league soccer for the club. He managed to keep going for 35 minutes before running out of steam, Wednesday playing the rest of the match with ten men, losing 2-0.

SATURDAY 27TH AUGUST 1983

New manager Howard Wilkinson gave debuts to four new players – Martin Hodge, Lawrie Madden, Chris Morris and Imre Varadi – as Wednesday won 1-0 (Lyons) at newly relegated Swansea City on the opening day of the season.

FRIDAY 27TH AUGUST 2004

The new controversial away fans ID scheme introduced by Wednesday failed its first test as Tranmere Rovers opened a cash turnstile for their League One game! The Wirral club won 4-2 with Wednesday's Guy Branston red carded.

SATURDAY 28TH AUGUST 1920

The club's first professional secretary-manager, Bob Brown, took charge of his first game – a 0-0 draw at Barnsley – on the opening day of the 1920/21 season.

SATURDAY 28TH AUGUST 1954

After losing their opening two games, the Owls beat Aston Villa 6-3 at Hillsborough. Albert Quixall opened the scoring after just four minutes and Wednesday were 5-1 ahead by half-time; Jackie Sewell and Jack Shaw netting two apiece. A late Alan Finney goal completed the scoring.

SATURDAY 28TH AUGUST 1999

It was 'taxi for Mr. Carbone' at The Dell, as the Owls' Italian forward walked out and flew home to Italy after Danny Wilson only named him as a substitute for the game against Southampton! The Owls lost 2-0 to remain bottom of the Premiership.

SATURDAY 29TH AUGUST 1931

The Owls made an astonishing start to the season, winning 6-1 at Blackburn Rovers. Inside-left George Stephenson led the way with four goals after Jack Ball and Mark Hooper had given Wednesday a 2-1 advantage at half-time.

SATURDAY 29TH AUGUST 1981

Wednesday won 1-0 at Blackburn Rovers on the opening day of the season, Terry Curran netting the winner after 37 minutes. The game also saw the debuts of both Gary Megson and Gary Bannister.

SATURDAY 30TH AUGUST 1924

Wednesday started the 1924/25 season as the first visitors to Selhurst Park – the new home of Crystal Palace. Due to industrial action the only stand in the ground was unfinished while an early goal from debutant Billy Marsden gave the Owls a 1-0 win.

SATURDAY 30TH AUGUST 1958

Wednesday won 2-0 at Ipswich Town in a Second Division fixture with Gerry Young and Roy Shiner netting. The success was the first away from home since December 29th 1956 – a run of 29 games.

SATURDAY 31ST AUGUST 1946

The fixtures from the aborted 1939-40 season were repeated when peacetime football returned in 1946, sending the Owls to Luton Town. The Hatters won 4-1 with the Owls scorer, Jackie Robinson, being the only player remaining from the 1939 team.

SATURDAY 31ST AUGUST 1968

In arguably the greatest game seen at Hillsborough, European Cup holders Manchester United were beaten 5-4, watched by 51,931 fans. A star-studded United side containing the likes of George Best and Bobby Charlton led 4-2 but Wednesday stormed back to win with a hat-trick from Jack Whitham, a goal from John Ritchie and an own goal from Nobby Stiles.

SATURDAY 31ST AUGUST 1991

England international Carlton Palmer was the most unlikely goalscoring hero as he grabbed a first half hat-trick as Queens Park Rangers were beaten 4-1 in a top flight game at Hillsborough.

SHEFFIELD WEDNESDAY
On This Day

SEPTEMBER

SATURDAY 1st SEPTEMBER 1894

The opening-day 3-1 defeat at Everton saw Tommy Crawshaw make his first team debut after signing from Manchester League club Heywood Central. Also new to the side was Bob Ferrier who had arrived from Dumbarton in the summer.

SATURDAY 1st SEPTEMBER 1900

Newly promoted Wednesday opened their season with a 2-2 draw at Manchester City. New signing Andrew Wilson made his debut with Jocky Wright scoring twice to secure the point.

SATURDAY 1st SEPTEMBER 1990

In the opening home game of the new season, David Hirst scored four times as Hull City were beaten 5-1 at Hillsborough to leave Wednesday top of the fledgling league table.

SATURDAY 1st SEPTEMBER 1993

After a poor start to the season the Owls looked set for their first win as goals from Chris Bart-Williams, Mark Bright and Andy Sinton put Wednesday 3-0 ahead after 62 minutes at Hillsborough. However, the Canaries hit back with three goals in just 13 minutes as the sides drew 3-3.

SUNDAY 1st SEPTEMBER 2002

New signing Lloyd Owusu made a dramatic debut from the subs' bench, scoring with his first touch in the 72nd minute, to put the Owls ahead in the Sheffield derby against the Blades. A second goal from Shefki Kuqi wrapped up a 2-0 win to give the blue and white half of the city 'bragging rights'.

FRIDAY 2nd SEPTEMBER 1887

John Edward 'Teddy' Davison was born in Gateshead. The diminutive 5ft 7ins. goalkeeper became a legend in Sheffield football, appearing in 424 games for the Owls and later managing the Blades for almost twenty years. He is also widely regarded as the shortest-ever goalkeeper to play for England. Davison won his only cap against Wales in March 1922.

SATURDAY 2ND SEPTEMBER 1899

A new era dawned at Wednesday as the club welcomed neighbours Chesterfield for the first-ever game at their new Owlerton ground. A crowd of 12,000 attended the Second Division fixture although the ground was very much a 'work in progress' with only the old 1,000 capacity Olive Grove Stand – which had been moved brick by brick from the club's old ground – providing any cover. The Lord Mayor kicked off the game and within a minute Harry Millar had fired against a post. However, it was Chesterfield player Herbert Munday who netted the first goal at the new ground. This proved only a minor setback as Wednesday stormed back to win 5-1 with a brace from Millar (64, 78) and goals from Fred Spiksley (33), Bob Ferrier (38) and Archie Brash (81).

SATURDAY 2ND SEPTEMBER 1939

With war looming, the Owls lost 1-0 at home to Plymouth Argyle in a Second Division fixture. Within days the Football League was closed down and the results of the first three games of the season were expunged.

MONDAY 2ND SEPTEMBER 1996

Wednesday maintained their 100% start to the season by beating Leicester City 2-1 at Hillsborough in front of the Sky TV cameras. A wonder goal from Ritchie Humphreys saw the Owls retain first place in the Premiership.

SATURDAY 3RD SEPTEMBER 1892

A goal from Tom Brandon secured a 1-0 win at Notts County in the club's first ever Football League game. A crowd of 10,000 were inside Meadow Lane to witness the historic first for Wednesday.

SATURDAY 3RD SEPTEMBER 1949

As post war crowds continued to rise the Owls were watched by 41,159 as Chesterfield were beaten 4-2 at Hillsborough. They saw Eddie Quigley score a hat-trick in just five minutes, either side of half-time, and then go on to score four goals in a single game for Wednesday for the second time in his Owls career.

WEDNESDAY 3RD SEPTEMBER 1952

A 41,183 Hillsborough crowd saw Tom McAnearney make his debut for the club but it was a losing start as Liverpool won 2-0.

TUESDAY 3RD SEPTEMBER 1985

The club's unbeaten start to the season ended in emphatic style as champions Everton won 5-1 at Hillsborough. Wednesday had actually taken the lead after 23 minutes, through a Brian Marwood penalty, but Trevor Steven, Gary Lineker and Adrian Heath were amongst the scorers as the Toffeemen silenced most of the 30,065 crowd.

WEDNESDAY 3RD SEPTEMBER 1989

Hillsborough staged its first ever rugby league game as Sheffield Eagles lost 36-20 to St. Helens in front of a 6,000 crowd.

WEDNESDAY 4TH SEPTEMBER 1867

At the Adelphi Hotel – where the Crucible Theatre now stands – a meeting was held to officially form a football section of the Sheffield Wednesday Cricket Club. Ben Chatterton was elected as president, John Marsh as secretary and team captain while colours of blue and white were adopted. Around sixty members were enrolled on the night, including many of the best players in Sheffield.

SATURDAY 4TH SEPTEMBER 1954

Jack Shaw was the first Wednesday man to be ordered off the field in a post-war league fixture after being dismissed, along with Sunderland's Stan Anderson, after the pair had to be pulled apart by the referee after a 'disagreement'. Sunderland won the game 2-0 in front of 52,112 fans, leaving Wednesday third from bottom in the top flight.

WEDNESDAY 4TH SEPTEMBER 1968

Just four days after the breathtaking win over Manchester United, the Owls were humbled 3-1 by Fourth Division Exeter City in a League Cup tie in Devon. An equaliser from David Ford after 55 minutes looked to have got the Owls back into the game but in front of 15,962 at St. James' Park, the home side netted twice more for a famous win.

TUESDAY 4TH SEPTEMBER 1979

Wednesday suffered late heartbreak in the League Cup at Manchester City after an 80th-minute penalty from Mark Smith put the Owls 2-1 ahead on aggregate in the second leg. However, City scored twice in the final two minutes to send Wednesday tumbling out of the competition.

SATURDAY 4TH SEPTEMBER 1999

In an FA Academy fixture at Middlewood Road, Wednesday and Crewe Alexandra drew 6-6 – the joint highest recorded draw, at any level, in the club's history.

SATURDAY 5TH SEPTEMBER 1891

Wednesday played foreign opposition for the first time, as a touring Canadian side were beaten 4-1 at Olive Grove. A hat-trick from 'Toddles' Woolhouse settled the game while goalkeeper Johnson was actually reserve goalie Docherty, playing under an assumed name.

FRIDAY 5TH SEPTEMBER 1924

An early part of the club's history was no more as The Wednesday Cricket Club was wound up.

SATURDAY 5TH SEPTEMBER 1931

Wednesday took their goals tally to 17 in the opening three games after Bolton Wanderers were thrashed 7-1 at Hillsborough. The visitors actually took the lead after seven minutes but the home side surged back to lead 3-1 at half-time and add four more in the second period.

SATURDAY 5TH SEPTEMBER 1987

It was a bittersweet day for Wednesday goalkeepers as Martin Hodge was forced to miss the game at Southampton due to injury – ending a club record run of 214 consecutive appearances. However, it was a great day for 19-year-old Kevin Pressman who made his debut in a 1-1 draw.

SATURDAY 6TH SEPTEMBER 1919

Wednesday were still searching for a first win of the season after a 3-0 defeat at Middlesbrough. The game was the farewell appearance of David McLean whose 100 goals in only 147 games – 88 in 135 First Division games – made him a candidate for the greatest number nine in the club's history.

SATURDAY 6TH SEPTEMBER 1947

In a Second Division fixture at Hillsborough, neighbours Barnsley were beaten 5-2 with centre-forward Jimmy Dailey scoring all five for Wednesday. He netted after 4, 42, 60, 68 and 87 minutes to join the select band of players to have achieved the feat in an Owls shirt.

WEDNESDAY 6TH SEPTEMBER 1967

The Owls celebrated their centenary at the home game against Fulham by charging half price or less to 26,551 fans that attended the game. The club also handed out commemorative pin badges and fittingly the subsequent 4-2 win left Wednesday top of the First Division table – one hundred years and two days after their formation.

SATURDAY 6TH SEPTEMBER 1980

Wednesday were involved in the wrong sort of headlines as so-called fans rioted in the game at Oldham Athletic, after favourite Terry Curran was sent off following a clash with Simon Stainrod. The game was held up for 27 minutes with the ten men eventually losing 2-0. After the incident, away fans were banned for the following three games while standing was closed at Hillsborough for the same number of games.

SATURDAY 7TH SEPTEMBER 1889

Wednesday played their first game in the Football Alliance League as Bootle were beaten 2-1 at Olive Grove with Billy Ingram scoring twice. After failing to gain admittance into the Football League, Wednesday were instrumental in forming the new Football Alliance League, which contained the likes of Newton Heath (Manchester United) and Nottingham Forest.

SATURDAY 7TH SEPTEMBER 1929

The 2-0 defeat to Arsenal at Hillsborough was the club's first home reverse since February 1928 – a run of 29 games without defeat.

TUESDAY 7TH SEPTEMBER 1971

On a disastrous night in Cumbria, the Owls crashed out of the League Cup at the second stage as fellow Second Division side Carlisle United handed out a 5-0 beating.

MONDAY 8TH SEPTEMBER 1930

Both Jack Ball and John Peacock made their Wednesday debuts as Chelsea drew 1-1 at Hillsborough. The careers of both players at Hillsborough differed greatly as Ball took the top division by storm. Peacock never played again for the Owls, coincidentally moving to Stamford Bridge in September 1930.

SATURDAY 8TH SEPTEMBER 1951

In front of 52,045 at Bramall Lane, Wednesday were quickly ahead as Keith Thomas scored his only goal for the club, netting after just 90 seconds. Unfortunately, it was all downhill from that point as the Blades hit back to lead 2-1 at half-time and then stunned Wednesday with a five-goal salvo, eventually winning 7-3 to record their best ever win over the Owls.

MONDAY 8TH SEPTEMBER 1952

In the club's first ever game in the newly introduced FA Youth Cup competition, Wednesday lost 3-2 to Hull City at Hillsborough. Amongst the scorers was Jim McAnearney who would graduate through the youth ranks to appear in 40 games for the senior side, netting 10 times, before being sold to Plymouth Argyle for £6,750 in January 1960.

MONDAY 8TH SEPTEMBER 1986

The Owls made the midweek trip to Kuwait to play a lucrative friendly against the national side, winning 5-2 thanks to goals from Colin Walker (2), Glynn Snodin, Brian Marwood and Lee Chapman.

WEDNESDAY 9TH SEPTEMBER 1931

Despite being 2-0 down after just 14 minutes the Owls recovered strongly at Chelsea to score either side of half-time to level the game and secure the two points thanks to a header from Ellis Rimmer.

SATURDAY 9TH SEPTEMBER 2000

The Owls suffered a second-half collapse at Hillsborough against Wimbledon in a First Division game. The match was 0-0 at the break but the Dons scored five goals without reply in the second period; John Hartson and Jason Euell each scoring twice.

SATURDAY 10th SEPTEMBER 1892

A bumper Olive Grove attendance of 12,000 saw Wednesday celebrate their first home game in league football by beating Accrington 5-2. The distinction of scoring the first home league goal fell to 'Sparrow' Brown while Fred Spiksley, Brown again, Harry Davis and 'Sandy' Rowan completed the rout.

WEDNESDAY 10th SEPTEMBER 1924

Norman 'Cannonball' Curtis was born at Dinnington, near Worksop. The left-back spent ten years on the Owls books, earning a reputation as a fearless, hard tackling player who scared many a budding wing wizard!

THURSDAY 10th SEPTEMBER 1936

Centre-forward Neil Dewar scored his second hat-trick in an Owls shirt, as Everton were beaten 6-4 at Hillsborough. After signing for Wednesday from Manchester United the Scot was at the centre of a scandal when he eloped with the daughter of a United director – the couple marrying in a registry office with the furore surrounding the incident eventually leading to the bride's father resigning from the United board! It would be the Scot's last season at Wednesday as he returned home to sign for Third Lanark in July 1937 after 50 goals in 97 games for the club.

WEDNESDAY 10th SEPTEMBER 1958

The Owls drew 3-3 at Sunderland with twin brothers, Derek and Eric Wilkinson, appearing together for the only time in their Wednesday careers – Eric's appearance being his only senior game for the club. In front of 33,684 fans, the away side led 3-1 but two late goals ensured honours were shared.

SATURDAY 11th SEPTEMBER 1909

Bristol City and Wednesday drew 1-1 at Ashton Gate in a First Division fixture. A 22nd-minute goal from Frank Bradshaw earned his side a point, after City had scored after ten minutes.

TUESDAY 11th SEPTEMBER 1979

In an entertaining Hillsborough testimonial for Paul Bradshaw, Wednesday beat Leeds United 4-2 with Roger Wylde scoring three for the Owls.

MONDAY 12TH SEPTEMBER 1887

Wednesday officially opened their new Olive Grove ground with a visit from Blackburn Rovers. Around 1,500 fans paid threepence each to see a thrilling 4-4 draw with Wednesday recovering from 4-1 in arrears to force a draw – Wednesday legend Fred Spiksley having the distinction of scoring the first goal at Olive Grove. The new ground was just off Queens Road in the centre of Sheffield and was just a swampy field when Wednesday signed a seven-year lease. In the summer of 1887 they spent £5,000 to bring the new ground up to standard – a large 'shed' was erected for 1,000 fans so Wednesday had reasonable facilities for a new era, having turned professional just a few weeks before.

SATURDAY 12TH SEPTEMBER 1925

It was another hat-trick for Jimmy Trotter as he grabbed four goals in a Second Division fixture at Hillsborough. On the receiving end on this occasion were Preston North End who netted a mere consolation in the final minutes as the Owls continued their pursuit of the Second Division championship with a 5-1 success, watched by 25,159.

TUESDAY 12TH SEPTEMBER 1961

The Owls first game in the Fairs Cup took them to French club Olympique Lyons where a crowd of 5,000 saw the home side win 4-2. Goals from Gerry Young and Keith Ellis had pulled Wednesday to within a goal of Lyon after the Frenchmen had surged into a 3-0 lead after 38 minutes. However, a last-minute strike from Nestor Combin left the Owls with a difficult second leg.

FRIDAY 13TH SEPTEMBER 1907

John Thomas Ball was born at Banks, near Southport. A lethal centre-forward, Jack Ball crashed home 94 goals for Wednesday in just 135 games, including 33 top flight goals in the 1932/33 season. His form was such that the outstanding Jack Allen, who Ball replaced, was hardly missed.

SATURDAY 13TH SEPTEMBER 2008

The Owls beat Watford 2-0 at Hillsborough – Marcus Tudgay and Tommy Spurr securing the three points.

SATURDAY 13TH SEPTEMBER 1919

A tramways strike hit the attendance at Hillsborough and those fans that did make the ground for the top flight meeting with Notts County probably had reason to regret the journey as the sides played out a drab 0-0 draw in pouring rain. Due to the conditions, the teams did not break for a half-time interval while Wednesday were still looking for their first win of the season after Jack Burkinshaw missed a first-half penalty.

TUESDAY 14TH SEPTEMBER 1948

Wednesday's youth side played their first-ever competitive fixture – winning 2-0 at local club Penistone Church, in the Hatchard League.

WEDNESDAY 14TH SEPTEMBER 1966

Wednesday played their first Football League Cup fixture as Rotherham United won 1-0 at Hillsborough thanks to a last-minute goal from Frank Casper.

WEDNESDAY 15TH SEPTEMBER 1976

Twenty-four hours after Wednesday announced a possible new share issue, the move was roundly criticised by fans with the President of the Shareholders association commenting; "The directors have proved they don't know how to spend money. Why should we give them any more?"

SATURDAY 15TH SEPTEMBER 2007

A 1-0 defeat at Preston North End meant the Owls had lost their first six games of the 2007/08 season – the worst start to a campaign in their history. The closest the Owls came was a curling attempt from Dutch winger Etienne Esajas that hit the post.

SATURDAY 16TH SEPTEMBER 1933

In his last game in charge, manager Bob Brown guided the Owls to a 3-0 home win over Middlesbrough. Goals from Mark Hooper, Ellis Rimmer and Jack Ball ensured it was a fitting finale for the legendary Wednesday manager.

MONDAY 16TH SEPTEMBER 1935

A late goal condemned Wednesday to their first home defeat for 17 months; Huddersfield Town won 2-1 at Hillsborough, watched by a 14,164 crowd.

DUTCH WINGER ETIENNE ESAJAS, SIGNED FROM VITESSE ARNHEM IN 2007

WEDNESDAY 16TH SEPTEMBER 1992

In their first European game since 1963, the Owls thrashed Luxembourg minnows Spora 8-1 at Hillsborough in a first round Uefa Cup tie. The night was overshadowed by an incident involving Paul Warhurst who, after colliding with the opposition keeper, was knocked unconscious and swallowed his tongue. Only the quick and decisive actions of physio Alan Smith saved his life – he spent several days in hospital before returning for the second leg.

SATURDAY 16TH SEPTEMBER 2000

Wednesday were forced to play in Tranmere Rovers' old away kit in a First Division game at Prenton Park, after the match referee changed his mind about the respective kits not clashing. The change of strip did not prove a lucky omen for the Owls as Rovers won 2-0 to leave Wednesday in the relegation places.

MONDAY 17TH SEPTEMBER 1888

In a practice game at Olive Grove the first team beat the reserves 5-0 although for some unknown reason both sides had only ten players!

WEDNESDAY 17TH SEPTEMBER 1958

The Second Division game with Sunderland ended in a 6-0 win for Wednesday as 'Red' Froggatt netted a second-half hat-trick in just ten minutes to add to first-half goals from Roy Shiner, Albert Quixall and Derek Wilkinson. The game proved to be 'Golden Boy' Albert Quixall's last appearance in an Owls shirt after 65 goals in 265 appearances – he moved to Manchester United for a British record fee of £45,000 just 24 hours later.

SATURDAY 18TH SEPTEMBER 1982

On Queens Park Rangers' synthetic pitch, goals from Andy McCulloch and Gary Bannister secured a 2-0 win to move the Owls into third place in the Second Division.

SATURDAY 18TH SEPTEMBER 2004

A scrappy 1-0 home defeat to AFC Bournemouth pushed the Owls into the bottom half of the League One table and ended the reign of boss Chris Turner.

SATURDAY 19TH SEPTEMBER 1931

The Owls continued their great start to the season by beating Huddersfield Town 4-1 at Hillsborough to record a fifth victory in six games from the start of the season.

SUNDAY 19TH SEPTEMBER 1999

The meeting of the bottom two of the Premiership had an unlikely outcome as bottom club Newcastle United thrashed Wednesday 8-0 with Alan Shearer scoring five times. Four goals in each half condemned Wednesday to one of the worst league defeats in their history.

SATURDAY 20TH SEPTEMBER 1969

After a poor start to the season, the Owls travelled to West Ham United, losing 3-0 with Harry Redknapp and Geoff Hurst amongst the scorers. The game also saw the final appearance of John Fantham in a Wednesday shirt, moving to Rotherham United for £4,000 soon after.

TUESDAY 20TH SEPTEMBER 2005

In an entertaining League Cup tie at Hillsborough, Premiership West Ham United won 4-2 although they were given a fright as goals from David Graham and Graham Coughlan brought Wednesday back into the tie after being 3-0 down.

MONDAY 21ST SEPTEMBER 1925

Jimmy Trotter scored five goals in a game for the second time as the Owls routed Stockport County 6-2 at Hillsborough. There was only going to be one winner after Trotter grabbed his first after 36 minutes – the centre-forward needed only 31 minutes to score his five.

THURSDAY 21ST SEPTEMBER 1933

Arguably the greatest manager in Wednesday's history, Bob Brown, tendered his resignation after over 13 years at the helm. The recent loss of his wife and poor health were the main reasons for the departure of a man who had led Wednesday during the golden period of their history.

SATURDAY 21ST SEPTEMBER 2002

Wednesday played their 2000th home league game but the meeting with Leicester City did not live long in the memory as the sides drew 0-0.

SATURDAY 22ND SEPTEMBER 1928

Wednesday's 5-2 win over Sheffield United remains the best derby result in league soccer. Two apiece from Jack Allen and Mark Hooper, plus one from Ellis Rimmer delighted the majority in a 44,699 Hillsborough crowd. The day was also significant as the new West Stand was used for the first time, boosting the ground capacity to around 80,000. Built by local contractors Freckingham and Sons, the new structure cost £7,233 but boasted covered terracing for 7,000 with a further 5,000 uncovered.

SATURDAY 22ND SEPTEMBER 1951

There were almost 55,000 inside Hillsborough to see the Second Division derby game against Rotherham United. The visitors raced into a 3-0 lead, eventually winning 5-3.

TUESDAY 22ND SEPTEMBER 1998

The delicious bacon sandwiches at the Abbey Stadium were no real consolation to Owls fans as the club tumbled out of the League Cup, 2-1 on aggregate after drawing 1-1 in the second leg.

WEDNESDAY 22ND SEPTEMBER 2004

Caretaker boss Mark Smith took charge of the Wednesday side as Coventry City won 1-0 at Highfield Road in a League Cup tie. The Owls played over half of the game with ten men after Glenn Whelan was sent off after 39 minutes.

SATURDAY 23RD SEPTEMBER 1933

Wednesday lost 3-1 at Blackburn Rovers in the First Division. However, the game was overshadowed by a double sending off with the Owls' Harry Burgess ordered off despite having seemingly been punched in the face!

SATURDAY 23RD SEPTEMBER 1950

Forward Derek Dooley reminded manager Eric Taylor of his qualities, scoring EIGHT as the club's 'A' team thrashed Halifax Town reserves 8-2.

SATURDAY 24TH SEPTEMBER 1949

Clarrie Jordan scored four as Hull City were thrashed 6-2 at Hillsborough. A gate of 52,869 was swelled by 10,000 from Hull; their supporters' club having made the game their chief outing of the season.

TUESDAY 24TH SEPTEMBER 1996

Wednesday crashed out of the League Cup at First Division Oxford United, losing 2-1 on aggregate after an 85th-minute goal from ex player Nigel Jemson.

SATURDAY 25TH SEPTEMBER 1909

A 3-0 defeat at Spurs left Wednesday bottom of the First Division with just two points from six games. The game also signalled the end of Willie Layton's first-team career at Wednesday – after retiring he became a pub landlord but left his wife and children in 1912 to emigrate to Australia.

WEDNESDAY 25TH SEPTEMBER 1963

Wednesday won 4-1 at Dutch club DOS Utrecht in a Fairs Cup tie – Eddie Holliday, Bronco Layne, John Quinn and a Mijnais own goal making the second leg a mere formality.

SATURDAY 25TH SEPTEMBER 1965

The Owls drew 0-0 at First Division new boys Northampton Town, the Cobblers only season in the English top flight.

SATURDAY 25TH SEPTEMBER 2004

New manager Paul Sturrock made a great start to life in the Hillsborough hot seat as he watched his new team win 3-0 at Wrexham – MacLean, Brunt and Proudlock on target.

SATURDAY 26TH SEPTEMBER 1959

After 96 goals in just 160 first-team appearances for Wednesday, Roy Shiner made his final appearance in a 2-0 home win over Luton Town. Shiner would move to Hull City for a £6,500 fee a few weeks later.

SATURDAY 26TH SEPTEMBER 1998

Wednesday attacker Paolo Di Canio had a 'slight disagreement' with referee Paul Alcock resulting in the official being pushed over by the fiery Italian after he had come to blows with Arsenal's Martin Keown. The pair were both sent off with the almost comical tumble by the referee effectively ending Di Canio's Hillsborough career; he never played again for the Owls after serving a lengthy ban. The controversy totally overshadowed a great last-minute strike from Lee Briscoe that secured a 1-0 win.

SATURDAY 27TH SEPTEMBER 2003

The goalkeeping injury crisis reached a nadir when coach Eric Nixon replaced Kevin Pressman after 29 minutes of the 0-0 home draw against Grimsby Town. He became the oldest post war player at 40 years, 358 days.

SATURDAY 27TH SEPTEMBER 2008

A superb Wade Small solo effort – his final goal in an Owls shirt – saw Wednesday come from a goal behind to win 2-1 at Charlton Athletic.

MONDAY 28TH SEPTEMBER 1908

The reserves drew 2-2 at home to Leicester Fosse but the game ended in farce. After being awarded a last-minute penalty, Jimmy Spoors struck the ball only for the referee to incredibly blow for full-time before it had reached the goal line! The game was ordered to be replayed by the Midland League although it is not known if the official's services were retained!

SATURDAY 28TH SEPTEMBER 1991

A terrific second-half header from John Harkes earned the Owls a deserved point as Liverpool were held to a 1-1 draw at Anfield.

FRIDAY 29TH SEPTEMBER 1916

Wednesday pre World War I hero Harry Chapman succumbed to tuberculosis, passing away at the tender age of just 38.

SATURDAY 29TH SEPTEMBER 1984

Wednesday recorded a terrific 2-0 win at Liverpool with goals from Imre Varadi and Gary Shelton. A few months after losing in a League Cup replay, Wednesday fans chanted "we said we'd be back and we are".

THURSDAY 30TH SEPTEMBER 1937

Wednesday were fined two guineas after they were found guilty of playing the unregistered Bob Curry at Aston Villa earlier in the month.

TUESDAY 30TH SEPTEMBER 1986

Thomas Spurr was born in Leeds. After graduating from the club's youth system, Tommy made his first-team bow in April 2006 and went on to become Wednesday's undisputed left-back.

SHEFFIELD WEDNESDAY
On This Day

OCTOBER

THURSDAY 1st OCTOBER 1936

Gerry Morton Young was born at Harton, South Shields. After signing part-time for Wednesday he completed his electrician apprenticeship and signed full-time forms in May 1955.

SUNDAY 1st OCTOBER 1961

Another successful product of the club's youth policy of the late 1970s, Mel Sterland was born on this day in Sheffield. After signing professional forms in October 1979 he would play 347 games for Wednesday, scoring 49 goals, earning the nickname of 'Zico' after the Brazilian star of the era.

SATURDAY 1st OCTOBER 1966

When the Owls were awarded a penalty in the 4-2 defeat at Southampton it was a momentous occasion as it had been an incredible 82 games since the last one!

THURSDAY 1st OCTOBER 1992

Wednesday fans almost outnumbered the home supporters in a 2,379 crowd as Spora were beaten 2-1 in Luxembourg to complete a 10-2 aggregate win in the Uefa Cup first round.

WEDNESDAY 2nd OCTOBER 1991

Despite around 1,000 Wednesday fans travelling for the midweek game against Wimbledon, at their temporary home at Selhurst Park, the game still set a new low (3,121) crowd figure for a post-war top flight game. The 'barmy army' would not have enjoyed the long journey home as the Dons won 2-1, Nigel Pearson netting the consolation.

SATURDAY 2nd OCTOBER 1999

Wednesday gained their first win of the new season in spectacular style, beating Wimbledon 5-1 at Hillsborough with Gilles De Bilde scoring twice – his first league goals in an Owls shirt.

WEDNESDAY 3rd OCTOBER 1984

Wednesday drew 1-1 against Halmstads BK in a friendly to celebrate the 80th birthday of the Swedish Football Association. A crowd of 5,252 watched the action and saw Lee Chapman equalise for the English visitors with twelve minutes remaining.

TUESDAY 3RD OCTOBER 1989

Four goals from Steve Whitton, three from Dalian Atkinson and a late strike from Craig Shakespeare completed the 8-0 rout of Aldershot in a League Cup tie at the Recreation Ground. The victory is the club's biggest away win of all time and followed a first leg that had incredibly finished 0-0!

WEDNESDAY 3RD OCTOBER 1990

The Owls continued their superb start to the season by winning 4-0 over Brighton & Hove Albion at the Goldstone Ground. Danny Wilson, John Sheridan, Paul Williams and Nigel Pearson netted to keep Wednesday in second place.

WEDNESDAY 4TH OCTOBER 1961

Over 30,000 were inside Hillsborough for the return tie with Lyons in the Fairs Cup and the game looked to be heading for extra time until, with five minutes remaining, John Fantham's diving header made the score 5-2 to Wednesday on the night and 7-6 on aggregate. Fantham had opened the scoring after nine minutes and further Owls goals came from Billy Griffin, Tom McAnearney (penalty) and Colin Dobson.

SATURDAY 4TH OCTOBER 1986

A 6-1 home win over Oxford United lifted Wednesday up to fourth place in the top flight with Carl Shutt, Lee Chapman and Mark Chamberlain amongst the scorers. John Aldridge scored a consolation for United.

SATURDAY 4TH OCTOBER 1997

It was an Italian job at Hillsborough as a brace from Benito Carbone and one from Paolo Di Canio secured a 3-1 win over Everton, with all the four goals being scored in the final twelve minutes of the top flight meeting. A substitute appearance from David Hirst proved to be his last hurrah after 358 games for Wednesday.

WEDNESDAY 4TH OCTOBER 1995

Mark Bright netted a hat-trick as Crewe Alexandra were beaten 5-2 in the League Cup second round, winning through to the next round by an aggregate of 7-4.

SATURDAY 5th OCTOBER 1912

On a disastrous afternoon at Villa Park, the Owls were crushed 10-0 to record their heaviest ever defeat in competitive football. Aston Villa forward Harry Hampton scored five for the home side, who led 6-0 at half-time, with the two points won that day enough for Villa to pip Wednesday to runners-up spot in the final First Division table, in what otherwise was an excellent season for the Owls.

WEDNESDAY 5th OCTOBER 1977

With Wednesday bottom of the old Third Division, manager Len Ashurst was sacked with coach Ken Knighton put in temporary charge of first team affairs.

MONDAY 6th OCTOBER 1986

Only 2,089 fans were at Maine Road to see the second leg of the second round League Cup tie between Stockport County and Wednesday. County had moved the game to Manchester City's ground in the hope of a bumper crowd but a 3-0 loss at Hillsborough in the first leg meant the return was virtually academic. The Owls took advantage to register a 7-0 win with Colin Walker becoming the only Wednesday player to score a hat-trick after entering the field as a substitute.

SATURDAY 6th OCTOBER 1990

The Owls met Bristol Rovers at their temporary home of Twerton Park, Bath with Trevor Francis grabbing the game's only goal to delight the rain sodden and wind blown Wednesday fans who had made the long trip.

WEDNESDAY 7th OCTOBER 1896

The club's officials and players enjoyed a lavish dinner at the Masonic Hall on Surrey Street to celebrate the winning of the English Cup. A huge menu included Mock Turtle soup, Jugged Hare, Apricot Creams and Gorgonzola cheese!

SATURDAY 7th OCTOBER 1961

Chelsea attacker Bobby Tambling netted a hat-trick at Hillsborough but finished the afternoon on the losing side as Wednesday recovered from 2-0 down to win 5-3 in a First Division encounter.

TREVOR FRANCIS — WEDNESDAY PLAYER AND MANAGER IN THE 1990S

WEDNESDAY 8TH OCTOBER 1930

Wednesday faced Arsenal at Stamford Bridge in the FA Charity Shield. Goals from Joe Hulme and David Jack put the Gunners in the driving seat and despite a late penalty from Harry Burgess, the London side lifted the trophy after a 2-1 win.

SATURDAY 8TH OCTOBER 1977

After a terrible start to their Third Division season, the Owls faced neighbours Chesterfield at Hillsborough still searching for their first win of the campaign. Thankfully a goal from Tommy Tynan was enough to claim that first win although Wednesday remained rooted to the foot of the division. However, the game was not remembered for the result, but for the appearance of Jack Charlton in the stands with the rumour mill suggesting he would be the club's next manager.

SATURDAY 8TH OCTOBER 1983

For once, the curse of the Manager of the Month award did not lead to immediate defeat as Howard Wilkinson received his bottle of whisky before watching his side beat Leeds United 3-1 at Hillsborough. Gary Shelton, John Pearson and Chris Morris netted for Wednesday.

SATURDAY 9TH OCTOBER 1937

The Owls' poor start to the 1937/38 campaign continued at Southampton where despite a brace from centre-forward Ernest Matthews, the Owls lost 5-2 in what proved to be Mark Hooper's final game in Wednesday colours.

THURSDAY 9TH OCTOBER 1947

Wednesday smashed their club transfer record when paying Bury £12,000 for inside-forward Eddie Quigley.

SATURDAY 10TH OCTOBER 1908

A crowd of around 14,000 was inside Hillsborough to see the debut of goalkeeper Teddy Davison, who had signed from Gateshead Town earlier in the year for £300. The new boy kept a clean sheet as Wednesday beat Bristol City 2-0 with goals from Frank Rollinson and Billy Lloyd. The win maintained the Owls' 100% home record and pushed Wednesday up to fourth place in the top flight.

MONDAY 10TH OCTOBER 1955

On a memorable night at Hillsborough, Wednesday fans were treated to the dazzling skills of Hungarian side Vasas Budapest who crushed the Owls 7-1. The visitors received a standing ovation from the 45,983 strong crowd who realised they had witnessed something special.

SATURDAY 10TH OCTOBER 1970

Hopes that Wednesday could bounce straight back into the top flight were certainly put to bed as a struggling Owls side lost 5-1 at home to Luton Town, Malcolm MacDonald scoring a hat-trick for the visitors to leave Wednesday down in 17th place in the Second Division.

WEDNESDAY 10TH OCTOBER 2001

Wednesday goalie Kevin Pressman was the hero of the League Cup tie against Crystal Palace at Hillsborough. The game finished 2-2 (Ashley Westwood and Tony Crane) after extra time before Pressman saved three penalties in the shoot out as the Owls progressed 3-1 on spot kicks.

FRIDAY 11TH OCTOBER 1946

Wednesday legend Jackie Robinson was sold to First Division Sunderland for £6,800. The outstanding inside-forward had been capped four times by England before the war and ended his playing days at Lincoln City in the early 1950s.

SUNDAY 11TH OCTOBER 1992

At the Greenport Stadium, Cape Town, Wednesday beat South African club Hellenic 2-1, during a whistle stop tour of the African country. A double from Paul Warhurst gave the Owls the win in front of 6,000 supporters.

SATURDAY 12TH OCTOBER 1867

Just a few weeks after forming, the club held its first practice game at Highfield (on the spot where the library currently stands) with the club's members providing the teams.

SATURDAY 12TH OCTOBER 1889

In a Football Alliance League fixture at Olive Grove, Crewe Alexandra scored four times but Wednesday won 6-4 in front of a 3,000 crowd.

WEDNESDAY 12th OCTOBER 1977

A new era started at Wednesday as Jack Charlton took charge for the first time – Wednesday agonisingly losing 2-1 at Exeter City to a last-minute goal from Harry Holman.

WEDNESDAY 12th OCTOBER 1988

With caretaker manager Peter Eustace in charge, Wednesday beat Blackpool 3-1 at Hillsborough in the second leg of a second round tie. Unfortunately, a 2-0 defeat in the first match meant the Owls exited the competition on the away goals rule.

SATURDAY 13th OCTOBER 1962

Visitors Nottingham Forest recovered from a two-goal deficit to draw 2-2 with Wednesday in a top flight fixture, Tony Kay and Bronco Layne having scored for the home side.

MONDAY 13th OCTOBER 1986

Most of the spectators in a 1,600 crowd were unsure of the final score as Wednesday beat Grimsby Town 9-3 at Blundell Park in a testimonial match for Kevin Moore. Dense fog shrouded the pitch throughout the game with Colin Walker scoring four times for the Owls.

FRIDAY 13th OCTOBER 1995

The Owls agreed to sell their unsettled Romanian Dan Petrescu to Chelsea for a £2.6m fee, exactly double the amount Wednesday paid to Italian club Genoa in August 1994.

SATURDAY 14th OCTOBER 1961

Wednesday's John Hickton scored nine times as non-league Stamford Youth Club were beaten 16-0 in an FA Youth Cup tie at Hillsborough.

MONDAY 14th OCTOBER 1996

Owls boss David Pleat set a new club record when he paid Inter Milan £3m for diminutive forward Benito Carbone. In almost four years at Hillsborough he netted 26 times in 107 appearances prior to joining Premiership Bradford City on a free transfer in 2000. He later played on loan for both Derby County and Middlesbrough before returning home to Italy, commanding an £800,000 fee when moving from Bradford to Como in July 2002.

SATURDAY 14TH OCTOBER 2006

A stunning injury-time volley from Chris Brunt gave the Owls a 2-1 win over Barnsley, in front of 28,687 at Hillsborough. The game will also be remembered for the half-time appearance of girl duo 'Twin' who belted out a rendition of a Slade song before turning to the away fans and gesturing in a very unladylike way! Sisters, Francine and Nicola Gleadall, later narrowly missed out on representing Britain in the 2009 Eurovision Song contest, after reaching the national final.

SATURDAY 15TH OCTOBER 1904

Wednesday won their seventh consecutive game from the start of the season, beating Stoke FC 3-0 at Owlerton. Goals from Andrew Wilson, Harry Chapman and George Simpson earned the points.

TUESDAY 15TH OCTOBER 1963

A hat-trick from Bronco Layne ensured the Owls reached the next round of the Fairs Cup after beating DOS Utrecht 4-1 on the night and 8-2 on aggregate.

WEDNESDAY 15TH OCTOBER 2003

Wednesday played their first-ever game in the Associate Members' Cup competition, drawing 1-1 at home to Grimsby Town after the Mariners had scored in the second minute. The Owls scored all five penalties in the shoot out with Kevin Pressman saving once to send Wednesday through 5-4 on spot kicks.

SATURDAY 16TH OCTOBER 1937

The crew of *HMS Sheffield* was among the 50,000+ crowd at Hillsborough as United won 2-0 to take the Sheffield derby honours. The game was also broadcast live across 'The Empire' on BBC Radio.

SATURDAY 16TH OCTOBER 1976

A 53rd-minute goal from Jeff Johnson was enough to end the unbeaten home record of hosts Reading and hand Wednesday their first away success since winning at Fulham in December 1974; a run of 35 league games and worst away drought in the club's history.

SUNDAY 16th OCTOBER 1994

The usually mild mannered Des Walker saw the red mist descend on this day as he was red carded after the final whistle, as the Owls won 2-1 at Ipswich Town, in a live Sky TV game. A last-minute goal from David Hirst had provided a dramatic end to the game before Walker was dismissed after head-butting Town's Simon Milton.

TUESDAY 16th OCTOBER 2001

Immediately after the 2-1 home defeat to Preston North End at Hillsborough, manager Peter Shreeves resigned, with Wednesday bottom of the First Division. He later managed Barnet in the Football Conference and now works as an assessor for the Premiership.

SATURDAY 17th OCTOBER 1931

On a foggy afternoon at Goodison Park, the Owls were all at sea as Everton scored seven second-half goals to win 9-3 in a First Division encounter. Leading the way for the Merseyside club with five goals was one of the greatest goalscorers in the history of the game – Dixie Dean – while the overwhelming majority of the 38,186 crowd went home happy as the Toffeemen took the score to nine.

TUESDAY 17th OCTOBER 2000

A single goal loss at Burnley was the club's eighth consecutive league defeat, setting a new record. The run was mercifully ended five days later when Birmingham City were beaten at Hillsborough.

MONDAY 18th OCTOBER 1893

Rumours that Harry Davis had died after the Sheffield derby game at the weekend were proven incorrect! The forward spent seven years at Wednesday, scoring 42 goals in 184 appearances and luckily – for historians – left just before Wednesday signed another player with the exact same name!

SATURDAY 18th OCTOBER 1890

Almost a year since Wednesday beat Crewe Alexandra 6-4 at Olive Grove in an Alliance League game, the Railwaymen paid a return visit and bizarrely won by exactly the same score!

SATURDAY 18TH OCTOBER 1958

Wednesday retained first position in the Second Division table as visitors Grimsby Town were thrashed 6-0 at Hillsborough. Almost 30,000 were inside Hillsborough to see the unfortunate Mariners defender Roy Player score into his own net not once, but twice, in the first half! After the benevolent defender had turned in crosses from Derek Wilkinson and Alan Finney, respectively, the Owls scored four themselves, clocking up a six-goal advantage just past the hour mark.

WEDNESDAY 18TH OCTOBER 2006

A calamitous night at Layer Road effectively cost Paul Sturrock his job as Owls boss; Wednesday losing 4-0 to Colchester United to leave them just outside of the Championship relegation zone.

SATURDAY 19TH OCTOBER 1867

Almost seven weeks after the club was formed their first ever game took place with Sheffield-based side Mechanics providing the opposition for a match played at Norfolk Park. A win by three goals and four rouges to nil gave the fledgling Wednesday a perfect start. The rouge was a short-lived rule which was used to decide a drawn game. At the time the goal was four yards wide and nine feet tall with two further 'rouge' posts being situated a further four yards from each 'goal' post.

MONDAY 19TH OCTOBER 1891

In a friendly game played at the Invicta Grounds, Plumstead, Wednesday beat relative new boys Royal Arsenal 8-1 – the Londoners had been formed only five years earlier in 1886.

SATURDAY 20TH OCTOBER 1928

The Owls won 4-0 at Bury in a First Division fixture with centre-forward Jack Allen continuing his scoring streak by netting all four goals. He netted after 2, 3, 57 and 61 minutes to follow his hat-trick against Birmingham City on the previous Saturday. In total the Newcastle-born player would score an outstanding 85 goals in only 114 appearances for Wednesday, winning two league championship medals, before moving to Newcastle United where he scored both goals as they won the FA Cup in 1932.

SATURDAY 20TH OCTOBER 1984

The Owls' great start to the season continued as Leicester City were beaten 5-0, lifting Wednesday to second place in the First Division. A hat-trick from Imre Varadi led the scoring with Andy Blair and John Ryan - his only goal for the club – completing the rout.

TUESDAY 20TH OCTOBER 1992

A David Hirst goal put the Owls ahead in their Uefa Cup tie in Germany against Kaiserslautern. However, Hirst was controversially sent off just before the interval and the home side pulled clear to win 3-1.

SATURDAY 21ST OCTOBER 1876

The Wednesday and Parkwood Springs played the first ever game in the newly introduced Sheffield Challenge Cup competition. Wednesday won 3-1 (Butler 2, Tomlinson) on the way to becoming the first winners. The cup is still played for today – the final being fittingly played at Hillsborough.

SATURDAY 21ST OCTOBER 2006

In the first of four games caretaker manager Sean McAuley would be in charge, the Owls won 3-2 at home to Queens Park Rangers. The club's Academy boss would lead Wednesday to ten points out of twelve during his time at the helm.

SATURDAY 22ND OCTOBER 1921

In a Second Division game against Bradford Park Avenue, at Hillsborough, the Owls raced into a two-goal half-time lead. At the break Wednesday changed into all white shirts, due to fading light, and despite conceding early in the second period they held on for victory.

SATURDAY 22ND OCTOBER 1932

The Owls recorded their first away win of the season with a 5-3 success at Wolverhampton Wanderers, centre-forward Jack Ball netting four and Ellis Rimmer one.

SATURDAY 22ND OCTOBER 1949

Winger Charlie Tomlinson scored what is believed to be the fastest goal in the club's history – netting after just 12 seconds in the 1-0 Second Division win at Preston North End.

MONDAY 22ND OCTOBER 1962

On a memorable Hillsborough night, Brazilian Pele was the star of the show as his Santos side won 4-2 in front of 49,058. A hat-trick from Coutinho was overshadowed by a perfect penalty from Pele while Billy Griffin and Bronco Layne scored for Wednesday.

SATURDAY 22ND OCTOBER 1988

History was made at the Dell as Southampton played Wallace brothers, Danny, Rodney and Raymond in the 2-1 loss to Wednesday. It is the only instance in post-war soccer that three siblings have appeared in the same side although the Owls stole some of the headlines as David Reeves hit a 60th-minute winner

SATURDAY 23RD OCTOBER 1920

A bittersweet day for Johnny McIntyre; he scored a 13th-minute penalty only to be sent off with 20 minutes remaining. To compound matters, future Owl Jack Whitehouse netted twice to give visitors Birmingham a 2-1 win.

MONDAY 23RD OCTOBER 1935

A goal from Neil Dewar after 48 minutes was enough for Wednesday to beat Arsenal 1-0 at Highbury to win the FA Charity Shield.

SATURDAY 23RD OCTOBER 1965

Sunderland lost 3-1 at Hillsborough with David Ford becoming the first used substitute in the club's history. The new rule had been introduced in the summer and fittingly it was the twelfth game of the campaign before Wednesday utilised the twelfth man – Ford replacing the injured Brian Hill after just eight minutes.

TUESDAY 23RD OCTOBER 1990

An injury-time header from Carlton Palmer earned Wednesday a 1-1 draw at Barnsley. The draw stretched their unbeaten start to the season to 12 games, leaving them just behind leaders Oldham Athletic.

SATURDAY 24TH OCTOBER 1953

Two goals each from Clarrie Jordan and Jackie Sewell put Wednesday 2-0 and 4-2 ahead in the game with Portsmouth but the top flight match ended 4-4 as the visitors came back strongly twice.

TUESDAY 24TH OCTOBER 1978

Goals from Brian Hornsby and John Lowey secured a 2-1 home win over Exeter City as Wednesday struggled to lift themselves out of the Third Division's lower reaches.

SATURDAY 25TH OCTOBER 1986

You could hear a pin drop at Hillsborough during the 2-2 draw against Coventry City when City keeper Steve Ogrizovic's 62nd-minute punt up field bounced over Martin Hodge and into the net, putting City 2-1 ahead.

WEDNESDAY 25TH OCTOBER 1989

In a dramatic finale to the League Cup tie at Derby County, Wednesday went ahead through a David Hirst penalty after 86 minutes, only for the Rams to score twice to snatch a win.

TUESDAY 26TH OCTOBER 1982

Despite leading 2-1 from the first leg, Wednesday were taken to extra time at Hillsborough in the second leg of a League Cup game against Bristol City. It needed a 110th-minute goal from Kevin Taylor to send the Owls through.

SATURDAY 26TH OCTOBER 1991

The home game with Manchester United proved to be Nigel Jemson's finest hour in a Wednesday shirt as his second-half brace saw the Owls come back to win 3-2 in a thrilling First Division game – watched by 38,260 fans.

TUESDAY 27TH OCTOBER 1987

Former player David Hirst came back to haunt Barnsley as he hit the 75th-minute winner as Wednesday won 2-1 at Oakwell, in a League Cup third round tie.

TUESDAY 27TH OCTOBER 1992

Wednesday beat Leicester City 7-1 at Hillsborough in a third round League Cup tie. Mark Bright (2), Gordon Watson (2), David Hirst, Nigel Worthington and Chris Bart-Williams sent the Owls into the last sixteen.

SATURDAY 28TH OCTOBER 1871

A friendly against the Mackenzie Club was abandoned after just 20 minutes when the ball burst and a replacement could not be found!

SATURDAY 28th OCTOBER 1961

In an incredible reserve game at Hillsborough, the Owls thrashed Barnsley 14-0 to record their biggest ever win in the Central League. Four men grabbed hat-tricks with Lockwood and Quinn both grabbing four apiece.

SATURDAY 29th OCTOBER 1932

With England in the middle of an unseasonal icy grip, the Owls' Central League game at Turf Moor, against Burnley, was abandoned after 75 minutes for the simple reason of extreme cold!

FRIDAY 29th OCTOBER 1965

Wednesday paid £35,000, to fellow top flight club Chelsea, for Scottish international forward Jim McCalliog. He scored 27 times in 174 games for the Owls before being sold to Wolves in 1969.

TUESDAY 29th OCTOBER 1985

The Owls were victims of a 'giant-killing' as Fourth Division Swindon Town won 1-0 at the County Ground to reach the last sixteen of the League Cup.

SATURDAY 30th OCTOBER 1954

For the second season in a row, the Owls were thrashed 6-0 at bogey ground Deepdale with Preston North End centre-forward George Higham netting three of the goals for the Lilywhites.

WEDNESDAY 30th OCTOBER 2002

After the Owls lost 1-0 to Millwall at Hillsborough, manager Terry Yorath was told by a female Wednesday fan: "You might be a nice fella, but resign, will you." He duly tendered his resignation with the Owls facing a third consecutive relegation fight.

TUESDAY 31st OCTOBER 1933

Alan Finney, one of only three Wednesday players to have appeared in over 500 games for the club, was born at Langwith, Nottinghamshire. His tally of 504 puts him third in the all-time appearance table.

TUESDAY 31st OCTOBER 1978

Brothers, Peter and Paul Shirtliff, both scored as the Owls youth team beat Sheffield United 2-1 at Hillsborough in the FA Youth Cup.

SHEFFIELD WEDNESDAY
On This Day

NOVEMBER

SATURDAY 1st NOVEMBER 1930

Wednesday remained in touch with the two leading clubs after beating visitors Sunderland 7-2. A first hat-trick from summer signing Jack Ball, and goals from Rimmer, Burgess, Hooper and Wilson completed the win in front of 19,299.

SATURDAY 1st NOVEMBER 1975

The Third Division game at Walsall was abandoned after 26 minutes as heavy rain waterlogged the pitch. The sides were deadlocked at 0-0 when the referee called a halt with 5,836 fans at Fellows Park sent home to dry off!

SATURDAY 1st NOVEMBER 1997

A 6-1 defeat at Manchester United sparked the end of David Pleat's reign as Wednesday boss. In front of 55,529 the Owls were 5-0 behind before Guy Whittingham netted a consolation goal, as Wednesday slipped to last place for the first time for eight years.

WEDNESDAY 1st NOVEMBER 2000

A crowd of over 32,000 were inside Hillsborough as Wednesday met United in a League Cup third round tie. A goal after just 10 minutes from Efan Ekoku put the Owls ahead but Michael Brown equalised to send the game into extra time. With eight minutes remaining Ekoku scored his second to clinch a place in the last sixteen for Wednesday.

SATURDAY 2nd NOVEMBER 1901

A goal from all-time record scorer Andrew Wilson after 20 minutes was enough to beat Sheffield United at Hillsborough in a top flight derby game.

THURSDAY 2nd NOVEMBER 1989

Wednesday paid Nottingham Forest £500,000 for midfielder John Sheridan. The former Leeds United player had fallen out of favour under the unpredictable Brian Clough but would enjoy the best years of his career after moving to Hillsborough.

SATURDAY 3rd NOVEMBER 1951

Wednesday won 6-0 at home to Notts County with Derek Dooley scoring five. The prolific centre-forward netted all his goals in the second half in front of a bumper 46,570 crowd.

SATURDAY 3RD NOVEMBER 1990

Watched by 34,845 fans, Hillsborough was virtually sold out as promotion-chasing Oldham Athletic and Wednesday shared four goals in a tremendous Second Division game. The Latics led 2-0 but two penalties from John Sheridan pulled the scores level.

THURSDAY 3RD NOVEMBER 1994

The Owls sent a side to officially open the new floodlights at Somerset Senior League side Cheddar. A crowd of 850 packed into the little ground to see a Richard Barker hat-trick as Wednesday won 6-1.

SATURDAY 4TH NOVEMBER 1882

Lincolnshire minnows Spilsby were thrashed 12-2 in an FA Cup tie at Bramall Lane with Bob Gregory becoming the first player in the club's history to score five times in one game; a crowd of 800 watched the proceedings.

SATURDAY 4TH NOVEMBER 1961

Goals from John Fantham, Keith Ellis and Tony Kay saw the Owls beat Manchester United 3-1 at Hillsborough. Meanwhile in Ballymena, Northern Ireland the Worthington family welcomed a new arrival, a little boy named Nigel.

SATURDAY 4TH NOVEMBER 1989

With new signings Phil King and John Sheridan in the side, Wednesday grabbed a much needed 1-0 win at Nottingham Forest, a Terry Wilson own goal after 80 minutes handing the Owls all three points.

WEDNESDAY 4TH NOVEMBER 1992

The Owls' Uefa Cup run came to an end as Kaiserslautern held Wednesday to a 2-2 draw at Hillsborough, progressing through to the third round by virtue of a 5-3 aggregate score. A memorable night had seen the Owls twice ahead through Danny Wilson and then John Sheridan, but the Germans came back twice to go through.

WEDNESDAY 5TH NOVEMBER 1958

The visit of Italian side Napoli to Hillsborough attracted a crowd of 29,589 with Wednesday putting the Naples club to the sword winning 6-0 with Norman Curtis scoring twice from the penalty spot.

SATURDAY 5TH NOVEMBER 1983

The 2-0 home win over neighbours Barnsley saw the Owls set a new club record of 15 games unbeaten from the start of the season – surpassing the previous record set in 1899. A Mark Smith header and Mel Sterland penalty kept the Owls clear at the top of the old Second Division table.

SATURDAY 6TH NOVEMBER 1937

A calamitous 4-1 defeat at Barnsley sent the Owls to the bottom of the Second Division and spelt the end of Billy Walker's reign at Hillsborough.

WEDNESDAY 6TH NOVEMBER 1963

Wednesday looked to be heading out of the Fairs Cup in Germany as Cologne led 3-0 at half-time. However, two goals from John Fantham in the last five minutes meant there was all to play for in the second leg in Sheffield.

MONDAY 6TH NOVEMBER 1967

Kevin Pressman was born at Fareham, Hampshire. He joined the Owls in November 1985 and in almost twenty years at Hillsborough recorded 478 appearances, placing Pressman fourth in the all-time list.

TUESDAY 6TH NOVEMBER 1973

On a humiliating night in west London, the Owls were beaten 8-2 by Queens Park Rangers in a third round League Cup tie. Wednesday were actually level at 2-2 just before the interval but Rangers hit five second-half goals to complete the rout.

MONDAY 6TH NOVEMBER 2006

Wednesday appointed Scunthorpe United manager Brian Laws as their new boss, on a three-year contract. He was joined by his former assistant Russ Wilcox.

SATURDAY 7TH NOVEMBER 1942

Wednesday went goal crazy in the Football League North home game against Mansfield Town, winning 9-1 with guest player Maynell Burgin grabbing four goals and Jackie Robinson three.

TUESDAY 7TH NOVEMBER 2000

A 3-1 win at Watford was enough to take the Owls out of the bottom three places in the First Division. Goals from Steve Haslam, Tony Crane and Alan Quinn secured the vital three points.

SATURDAY 8TH NOVEMBER 1924

At the Old Recreation Ground, Wednesday lost 1-0 to a late goal from Port Vale attacker Wilf Kirkham. A poor game was best remembered for the two dogs that invaded the pitch in the first half, stopping play for a while, much to the amusement of the locals.

MONDAY 8TH NOVEMBER 1937

With Wednesday in dire straits at the bottom of the Second Division, manager Billy Walker resigned from his post. The former Aston Villa and England captain 'fell on his sword' after an extremely heated meeting with a group of angry shareholders!

SATURDAY 8TH NOVEMBER 1997

Caretaker boss Peter Shreeves made the job of management look easy as he watched Wednesday crash five first-half goals past Bolton Wanderers at Hillsborough – Andy Booth grabbing a hat-trick inside fifteen minutes. There was no further scoring in the second half with the three points moving Wednesday out of the bottom three in the Premiership.

MONDAY 9TH NOVEMBER 1953

Dressed in a 'floodlit special' kit of blue silk shirts with white arms, Wednesday lost 3-1 at Derby County in the club's first game under floodlights in the UK.

SATURDAY 9TH NOVEMBER 1974

One of only five wins in the whole 1974/75 season came on this day – 3-0 v. York City at Hillsborough. However, the game lived longer in the memory due to the appearance of a male streaker, wearing only his socks, shoes and glasses, who raced onto the pitch and gleefully smacked the ball past Owls goalkeeper Peter Springett! He was duly led away by a policeman who covered his 'embarrassment' with his helmet!

SATURDAY 9TH NOVEMBER 1985

There were 48,105 fans inside Hillsborough as Wednesday met a Ron Atkinson-led Manchester United side that were unbeaten and seemingly running away with the championship. On a tumultuous afternoon, the 'Hillsborough roar' spurred the Owls to a 1-0 win, Lee Chapman heading home a Mark Chamberlain corner after 84 minutes to take the spoils.

SATURDAY 9TH NOVEMBER 2002

New manager Chris Turner must have quickly realised he had a big job on his hands as Wednesday were comprehensively beaten 3-0 at Norwich City, in his first match in charge. The game was level at 0-0 but then Shefki Kuqi was red carded for handling on the line and City scored from the resultant penalty kick.

SUNDAY 9TH NOVEMBER 2003

Wednesday beat Southern League Salisbury City 4-0 in an FA Cup first round tie at Hillsborough on Remembrance Sunday. A hat-trick from Adam Proudlock helped to overcome the non-league side.

THURSDAY 10TH NOVEMBER 1938

At the inquest into the tragic death of a cyclist, the motorist involved – Owls player Len Massarella – was cleared of any blame after it was described how the Doncaster man had swerved into Massarella's path.

SATURDAY 10TH NOVEMBER 1962

The Owls drew 0-0 with Aston Villa but the Hillsborough natives revolted after star forward Bronco Layne was sent off after 65 minutes, following a clash with Jimmy MacEwan. Several fans ran onto the pitch to protest and cushions rained down from the North Stand!

FRIDAY 11TH NOVEMBER 1966

Wednesday set a new record transfer figure when they paid £80,000 for Stoke City's prolific centre-forward John Ritchie. He scored 45 times for the Owls, in 106 games, before being sold back to Stoke for £27,500 in July 1969.

SATURDAY 11TH NOVEMBER 2006

New manager Brian Laws made a perfect start to his Hillsborough career as goals from Marcus Tudgay and Madjid Bougherra secured a 2-0 win at Ipswich Town.

SATURDAY 12TH NOVEMBER 1904

In an incredible game at Owlerton, Wednesday came back from a 5-1 half-time deficit to claim an improbable point in a 5-5 draw. All had looked lost but second-half goals from Jimmy Stewart, George Simpson and Vivian Simpson pulled the score back to 5-4 before the 12,500 fans erupted when Bob Ferrier netted a last-gasp equaliser.

SATURDAY 12TH NOVEMBER 1960

Arguably the game of the 1960/61 season took place at Hillsborough as second-placed Wednesday met runaway First Division leaders Tottenham Hotspur. Work on the new cantilever North Stand meant Hillsborough was a three-sided ground and there is no doubt the club's record league crowd would have been severely threatened if four sides had been in use as 56,363 somehow managed to squeeze into the three sides! They witnessed a classic game as a 68th-minute strike from John Fantham clinched a 2-1 win to cut Spurs' lead at the top to five points.

WEDNESDAY 12TH NOVEMBER 2003

A terrific stoppage-time winner from Michael Reddy secured a 1-0 Associate Members' Cup win over Barnsley at Hillsborough, watched by a 13,575 crowd.

SATURDAY 13TH NOVEMBER 1920

The Owls remained in the lower reaches of the Second Division table as West Ham United centre-forward Syd Puddefoot scored all of his side's goals in the 4-0 win in East London.

SATURDAY 13TH NOVEMBER 1943

Howard Wilkinson was born in Sheffield. He would play 22 times for Wednesday but is best remembered for his spell as manager in the 1980s when the Owls regained their First Division place. He joined the Owls for a third spell in January 2009, working free of charge on a consultancy basis.

SATURDAY 14TH NOVEMBER 1942

Mansfield Town players must have been quite relieved when they had completed their Football League (North) fixtures against the Owls in the 1942/43 wartime season as a week after beating them 9-1 at Hillsborough, Wednesday won 10-2 at Field Mill with Jackie Robinson and guest player Maynell Burgin recording hat-tricks.

SATURDAY 14TH NOVEMBER 1959

After adapting to his new left-back role, Don Megson made his debut for Wednesday in the 1-1 draw against Burnley at Hillsborough. He would spend almost ten years as first choice in that position, amassing 442 appearances for the club.

SATURDAY 14TH NOVEMBER 1987

The 2-0 home defeat to Luton Town would have been long forgotten but for the penalty kick Wednesday were awarded three minutes from the break. It was taken by Colin West who blasted the ball so far over the bar that legend says it is still heading for the stars!

SATURDAY 14TH NOVEMBER 1998

Goalkeeper Pavel Srnicek made his Wednesday debut against his old club, Newcastle United, on this day. He helped the Owls gain a 1-1 draw in a game that was halted briefly in the second half when a female streaker ran onto the pitch. The Czech keeper appeared in 52 games for the Owls and now runs a goalkeeping school back in his native land.

SATURDAY 15TH NOVEMBER 1884

In a friendly played at the Parkside Grounds in Nottingham, Wednesday beat Nottingham Forest 5-0. Both sides were still strictly amateur in those days with only around 500 fans in attendance.

SATURDAY 15TH NOVEMBER 1924

A brace from centre-forward Jimmy Trotter clinched a 2-0 Hillsborough win over Middlesbrough. On the same day, on the Isle of Wight, future Wednesday scoring hero Roy Albert James Shiner was born.

SATURDAY 16TH NOVEMBER 1889

In an Alliance League fixture at Olive Grove, the Owls maintained their 100% home record with a 9-1 thrashing of Long Eaton Rangers – Billy Ingram netting four goals.

SATURDAY 16TH NOVEMBER 1929

Wednesday put Manchester United to the sword at Hillsborough in a top flight fixture with Jack Allen grabbing four goals in a 7-2 win. An Ellis Rimmer brace and a Mark Hooper goal pushed the Owls into second place, on the coat-tails of leaders Manchester City.

SATURDAY 16TH NOVEMBER 1963

In an action packed top flight game, Stoke City and the Owls shared eight goals at the Victoria Ground with Wednesday recovering from 3-0 and 4-2 behind, thanks to two goals apiece from Bronco Layne and Mark Pearson.

SATURDAY 17TH NOVEMBER 1979

Wednesday attacker John Lowey scored four times as the reserve team won 5-4 at Blackpool in an entertaining Central League game.

WEDNESDAY 17TH NOVEMBER 1993

New Wednesday signings, Des Walker and Andy Sinton, played in England's 7-1 romp over minnows San Marino. It proved to be Walker's final cap for his country.

SATURDAY 18TH NOVEMBER 1893

With Wednesday leading 3-1 against Stoke in a top flight game the referee abandoned the match with just 20 minutes remaining, after claiming he could not see the ball as heavy snow engulfed Olive Grove. The 1,500 hardy souls who had braved the arctic conditions were not amused!

SATURDAY 18TH NOVEMBER 2006

For the first time, the Owls had two players sent off in a league game. Both Wade Small and Chris Brunt were shown red cards at Coventry City. Wednesday took the lead with just ten men but when Brunt was red carded just before the break the game swung towards the home side, who registered a 3-1 win.

SATURDAY 19TH NOVEMBER 1938

History was made at Hillsborough as Doug Hunt entered the record books as the only Wednesday player to have scored a double hat-trick in a competitive fixture. He scored after 17, 25, 39, 44, 65 and 87 minutes as Norwich City were beaten 7-0 in a Second Division fixture. A week later he scored three in a 5-1 win at Luton Town and during eight years at Wednesday – the majority lost to the Second World War – the Hampshire-born centre-forward netted 31 goals in 48 appearances before ending his playing days at non-league Gloucester City.

SATURDAY 19TH NOVEMBER 1949

The Second Division game at Coventry City kicked off in foggy conditions and slowly deteriorated to such an extent that when home player Roberts went off for treatment it took him several minutes to find the referee to get back on! Eventually the official called a halt to proceedings, abandoning the game after 63 minutes with City leading 1-0 through a Roberts goal after two minutes.

TUESDAY 19TH NOVEMBER 1957

Hero of the Owls back-to-back league titles in the late 1920s, Jack Allen, died at Burnopfield, County Durham. In only four years at Wednesday the lethal centre-forward netted 85 times, including 33 league goals in both championship seasons. Inconceivably to modern eyes, he spent the whole of the 1930/31 season in the reserves after Wednesday bought Jack Ball – Wednesday refusing to adapt their rigid 2-3-5 formation to accommodate both of the prolific marksmen!

SATURDAY 20TH NOVEMBER 1971

A 75th-minute headed goal from Brian Joicey earned Derek Dooley's Wednesday side a point in the 1-1 Second Division draw with Norwich City at Hillsborough.

TUESDAY 20TH NOVEMBER 1984

History was made at Hillsborough when midfielder Andy Blair became the first man to score a hat-trick of penalties in one League Cup game. He netted from the spot after 15, 51 and 70 minutes as Wednesday beat Luton Town 4-2, to reach the last eight of the competition.

WEDNESDAY 20TH NOVEMBER 1991

The Owls' grasp of the League Cup ended at The Dell as a 69th-minute goal from Barry Horne handed Southampton a 1-0 win, to knock the holders out in a third round replay, after a 1-1 draw at Hillsborough.

FRIDAY 21ST NOVEMBER 1941

One of the finest players of the club's early years, Jack Hudson, died in Worksop. He appeared in 16 FA Cup ties for Wednesday including their first-ever game in the tournament plus their first semi-final appearance in 1882. During a brief spell as club secretary in 1886 he made the error of forgetting to enter Wednesday into that season's FA Cup! After being instrumental in helping Wednesday turn professional he later played in Sheffield United's first ever game before returning to coach the Owls during the Olive Grove years.

TUESDAY 21ST NOVEMBER 1989

The much maligned Full Members' Cup got a shot in the arm as 30,464 were inside Hillsborough for the derby clash with Sheffield United – the largest attendance in the history of the short-lived tournament for a game played outside of Wembley. The fans saw a thriller as Wednesday led twice, through Dalian Atkinson, and then Carlton Palmer, only for the Blades to level twice, equalising in the final minute. A wonder goal from John Sheridan settled the game after 94 minutes as he ran from the centre circle before firing home from 20 yards.

SATURDAY 21ST NOVEMBER 1998

Watched by 39,475 at Hillsborough, Wednesday recorded a 3-1 win over Manchester United, Niclas Alexandersson (2) and Dutchman Wim Jonk netting for the Owls.

SATURDAY 22ND NOVEMBER 1975

Wednesday had to start in the first round of the FA Cup for the first time since joining the Football League in 1892. Visitors to Hillsborough were Northern Premier League Macclesfield Town who went in at the interval all square at 1-1. Chances of an upset were snuffed out in the second period as Wednesday scored through Ken Knighton and Mick Prendergast.

SATURDAY 22ND NOVEMBER 1997

The return of Ron Atkinson as Wednesday boss boosted the Hillsborough crowd to 34,373, for his first game in charge against Arsenal. Goals from Andy Booth and Guy Whittingham ensured a winning return for 'Big Ron'.

SATURDAY 23RD NOVEMBER 1991

New 17-year-old signing Chris Bart-Williams was outstanding on his debut as David Hirst and Steve Bould netted in a 1-1 draw against Arsenal at Hillsborough. The Owls had signed the youngster from Leyton Orient for a £575,000 fee with Chris Turner going in the opposite direction as part of the deal. The 'Bartman' scored 24 goals during his time at Wednesday, in 156 games, and the Owls received a transfer tribunal set £2.5m when he left for Nottingham Forest in the summer of 1995.

WEDNESDAY 23RD NOVEMBER 1994

The popularity of Chris Waddle was shown when over 3,500 turned out at Millmoor – the Owls venue for their reserve games – to see his comeback. The second team won 2-0 against Manchester City to complete the evening.

THURSDAY 24TH NOVEMBER 1927

Wednesday signed centre-forward Ted Harper from Blackburn Rovers for a club record £4,400 fee. He scored 16 goals in only 22 games before being sold to Spurs for a £600 profit in March 1929.

SATURDAY 24TH NOVEMBER 1990

In a dramatic finish at the Hawthorns, Wednesday scored twice (Trevor Francis and Peter Shirtliff) in the final five minutes to snatch a 2-1 win against West Bromwich Albion as the Owls continued to fly high near the top of the Second Division.

SATURDAY 25TH NOVEMBER 1882

Wednesday used Robert's Farm, situated just off Hunter's Bar, for the first time. Local side Thurlstone were beaten 5-0 in a friendly match with Herbert Newbould (2), Cawthorne, Chas Stratford and Jack Bingley netting to give the club a perfect start in their new home.

SATURDAY 25TH NOVEMBER 1899

Prolific 1920s centre-forward, James William Trotter, was born in Easington. His career started at Bury before he hit the heights at Wednesday, scoring an astonishing 37 league goals in 1925/26 as the Owls lifted the Second Division championship.

SATURDAY 25TH NOVEMBER 1950

Wednesday handed Norman Curtis a debut at left-back and the 37,033 Hillsborough crowd saw a seven-goal bonanza as visitors Bolton Wanderers won 4-3; leaving the Owls second from bottom in the First Division.

FRIDAY 25TH NOVEMBER 1960

At the grand old age of 87, FA Cup winning captain Tommy Crawshaw passed away in Wharncliffe Hospital, Sheffield. After retiring from the game he ran a newsagents on Bramall Lane (!) and then worked as a publican in Sheffield.

TUESDAY 25TH NOVEMBER 1986

The Owls debut in the new Full Members' Cup competition did little to rouse interest with only 7,846 inside Hillsborough to see Portsmouth win 1-0 in a poor game.

SATURDAY 26TH NOVEMBER 1927

In an incredible game at Derby County, Wednesday found themselves 3-1 in arrears at the interval before scoring three times in as many minutes early in the second half to lead 4-3. Although County equalised a minute after Wednesday went ahead it would be the Owls who took the points after scoring twice more to wrap up a 6-4 win – a Ted Harper hat-trick helping move his struggling side up out of the relegation zone.

SATURDAY 26TH NOVEMBER 1955

A late penalty from Roy Shiner rescued a point from the home game with West Ham United in Jackie Sewell's final game for Wednesday, after 92 goals in 175 first-team games. After spells at Hull City and Aston Villa, Sewell later played and coached in Zimbabwe (then called Rhodesia) before returning home in the early 1970s to work as a car salesman back in Nottingham.

FRIDAY 26TH NOVEMBER 1965

Desmond Sinclair Walker was born in Hackney, London. The lightning quick central defender would spend a total of 17 years at Forest, and then Wednesday, winning 58 caps for England.

WEDNESDAY 27TH NOVEMBER 1963

In front of 36,929 at Hillsborough, Wednesday made a great start to their second leg Fairs Cup tie against Cologne when Bronco Layne scored after 17 minutes to level the tie at 3-3. Unfortunately, second half goals from Thielen and Overath sent Wednesday out after they were beaten 2-1 on the night.

SATURDAY 27TH NOVEMBER 2004

A brace from Adam Proudlock helped Wednesday to a 4-1 win at promotion rivals Bristol City. Winger Chris Brunt also netted while youngster Patrick Collins scored his only goal for the club. The game would be remembered for all the wrong reasons by an unfortunate Owls fan that was hit full in the face by a clearance from Brunt. The supporter fell onto the concrete headfirst and had to be taken to hospital, being released later after treatment.

THURSDAY 28TH NOVEMBER 1929

The first meeting of the newly formed Sheffield Wednesday Supporters Club was held in the city.

SATURDAY 28TH NOVEMBER 1959

The Owls surge up the First Division table continued at a pace as West Ham United were beaten 7-0 at Hillsborough with five different Wednesday players finding the netting; John Fantham (2), Alan Finney (2), Derek Wilkinson, Bobby Craig and Keith Ellis. A crowd of 38,307 watched as their favourites moved up to ninth place.

SATURDAY 28TH NOVEMBER 1964

Wednesday managers Billy Walker (1933-37) and Jimmy McMullan (1938-42) both passed away on this day. The former took the Owls to the FA Cup in 1935 while McMullan led the club through the early years of wartime football before leaving football altogether to work in industry for the remainder of his life.

WEDNESDAY 28TH NOVEMBER 2001

A first-half goal from Efan Ekoku earned the Owls a shock 1-0 League Cup fourth round win at Premiership Aston Villa.

SATURDAY 29TH NOVEMBER 1884

On a disastrous afternoon, an under strength Wednesday side were beaten 12-0 at Blackburn Olympic in a friendly fixture.

SATURDAY 29TH NOVEMBER 1930

For the second time in the month, the Owls scored seven at Hillsborough with the victims on this occasion being Blackpool, who returned to Lancashire on the receiving end of a 7-1 beating. The game was effectively won early on. After just 21 minutes Mark Hooper had a hat-trick and Wednesday were four goals ahead. The two points kept the Owls in second place, just behind leaders Arsenal.

WEDNESDAY 29TH NOVEMBER 1961

Italian opponents AS Roma were beaten 4-0 at Hillsborough in the first leg of a Fairs Cup second round tie. A bumper crowd of 42,589 enjoyed a classic European night with Gerry Young scoring three times to virtually kill the tie at the first attempt.

WEDNESDAY 29TH NOVEMBER 2000

First-half goals from Owen Morrison and Ashley Westwood were enough to send Wednesday into the quarter finals of the League Cup, after beating top flight West Ham United 2-1 at Upton Park.

SATURDAY 30TH NOVEMBER 1974

Wednesday continued to struggle at the wrong end of the Second Division, losing 1-0 to Portsmouth at Fratton Park, who also missed a first-half penalty.

SATURDAY 30TH NOVEMBER 1872

Wednesday player, and future chairman, Charles Clegg played for England in the first-ever international fixture; a 0-0 draw against Scotland in Glasgow.

SHEFFIELD WEDNESDAY
On This Day

DECEMBER

SUNDAY 1st DECEMBER 1935

The match ball was bizarrely dropped from an aeroplane two minutes before the start of the Owls friendly against a French League select side in Lille. Wednesday had travelled overnight to France and then played on a quagmire of a pitch. The French side contained players from Poland, England, Spain and France and won 3-2 in front of a record 19,000 crowd with Dewar scoring twice for Wednesday.

SATURDAY 1st DECEMBER 1990

Wednesday fans saw the strange sight of their side wearing their yellow and blue away kit for the 2-2 home draw against Notts County. The referee had decided that both of County's strips clashed with Wednesday's traditional blue and white so they had no option but to play in away colours.

SATURDAY 2nd DECEMBER 1882

In front of 1,300 fans, The Wednesday moved into the next round of the FA Cup by winning 6-0 at local rivals Lockwood Brothers, the cup-tie being played at the home side's Eccleshall Road pitch.

SATURDAY 2nd DECEMBER 1899

Wednesday continued their unbeaten start to the 1899/00 season, as Luton Town were beaten 6-0 with Fred Spiksley grabbing a hat-trick. The win kept the Owls in pole position in the Second Division on a day when Wednesday donated 20% of the gate receipts to the Lord Mayor's fund for Army Reservists' wives and children.

SATURDAY 2nd DECEMBER 2000

A hat-trick from Dutch striker Gerald Sibon helped Wednesday to beat Queens Park Rangers 5-2 at Hillsborough. A crowd of 21,782 saw Owen Morrison and Efan Ekoku also net for Wednesday while a youngster called Peter Crouch scored twice for QPR.

SATURDAY 2nd DECEMBER 2006

In a game of spectacular goals, Wednesday recorded their first win at Leicester City's new Walkers Stadium. Long-range efforts from Chris Brunt, Glenn Whelan and Marcus Tudgay helped seal an outstanding 4-1 win.

SATURDAY 3RD DECEMBER 1932

Wednesday recorded their fourth consecutive win – beating Aston Villa 6-3 at Villa Park – to move into the First Division's top three. Villa, who had previously won every home game, lost that record in spectacular style.

FRIDAY 3RD DECEMBER 1948

Wednesday set a new British transfer record when they paid Bury £20,000 for the services of highly rated winger Eddie Kilshaw. Sadly, he appeared in only 19 games for the Owls before his career was ended after snapping his cruciate knee ligament in a game against Leicester City in April 1949.

SATURDAY 3RD DECEMBER 1955

In a Second Division game at Craven Cottage, the Owls won 2-1 but had to thank Fulham left winger Charlie Mitten who hit a post with a last-minute penalty given for handball.

SATURDAY 4TH DECEMBER 1993

Watched by a Hillsborough crowd of 32,177, Wednesday beat Liverpool 3-1 in the Premiership. The Owls were grateful to visiting defenders Neil Ruddock and Mark Wright who both scored past Bruce Grobbelaar with Mark Bright adding a third for the home side.

MONDAY 4TH DECEMBER 1995

Visiting forward Dion Dublin netted three times for Coventry City, in a live Sky TV game at Hillsborough, but still finished on the losing side as Wednesday came from behind on three occasions before Mark Bright clinched a 4-3 win.

SATURDAY 5TH DECEMBER 1925

Wednesday and Clapton Orient played out a 0-0 draw at Brisbane Road on a pitch that was so hard that many of the players wore knee bands to protect their joints!

SATURDAY 5TH DECEMBER 1959

The Owls won 4-0 at Chelsea with John Fantham (2), Bobby Craig and Keith Ellis netting for Wednesday. Also on this day in Lincoln, Lee Chapman was born. The no nonsense striker would net 78 times for the club in 187 appearances between 1984 and 1988.

SUNDAY 5TH DECEMBER 1999

The 4-1 Premiership defeat at Liverpool was perhaps more memorable for the half-time entertainment with newly formed band Atomic Kitten being given an early public airing. In true away fan style, the Wednesday away following booed all the way through to show their appreciation!

THURSDAY 6TH DECEMBER 1956

The Owls drew 1-1 with Yugoslavian visitors Zagreb in a Hillsborough friendly. However, the game became rather unfriendly – mainly due to countless body checks from the visiting side – and during the second half a fan was heard to shout "put out the lights and let them have a proper go".

SATURDAY 6TH DECEMBER 1975

Despite leading through an Eric Potts goal, Wednesday lost 2-1 at Colchester United to leave them in 21st place in the Third Division.

THURSDAY 7TH DECEMBER 1967

David Eric Hirst was born in Cudworth, Barnsley. His career started at his hometown club in 1985 before scoring 128 goals for Wednesday in 11 years at Hillsborough – leaving Hirst the sixth highest goalscorer in the Owls' history.

SATURDAY 7TH DECEMBER 1996

Wednesday fans enjoyed a great away day at Anfield as a goal from Guy Whittingham, after 21 minutes, secured a 1-0 top flight win over Liverpool.

FRIDAY 8TH DECEMBER 1933

After over ten weeks of deliberation, Wednesday made the surprise appointment of Billy Walker as manager. He was one of the best players of his generation, winning 18 caps for England and scoring 244 times in 531 games for his only club, Aston Villa.

SATURDAY 8TH DECEMBER 1951

With Derek Dooley on fire, the Owls won 6-0 at West Ham United, the centre-forward netting a first-half treble in 27 minutes. A brace from Redfern Froggatt and one from Albert Quixall completed the scoring on a memorable afternoon for half-back Len Edwards who was handed his first-team debut by manager Eric Taylor.

SATURDAY 8TH DECEMBER 1984

A 1-1 home draw with Chelsea marked the Owls' 2,000th top flight game. A late strike from Imre Varadi earned a point in front of a 29,373 crowd.

SATURDAY 8TH DECEMBER 2007

The Championship game with Coventry City was abandoned after 28 minutes with the Hillsborough pitch waterlogged after a deluge of heavy rain. The score was 0-0 at the time.

SATURDAY 9TH DECEMBER 1933

New manager Billy Walker took charge for the first time as Wednesday recorded a welcome 3-1 win at Liverpool, keeping the Owls out of the relegation places. Walker had the unenviable task of following in the footsteps of the club's greatest ever manager, Bob Brown, and did achieve success before the club was relegated in 1937.

SATURDAY 9TH DECEMBER 1967

With Arsenal leading through a Frank McLintock goal after nine minutes, the referee called a halt to play as heavy snow created blizzard conditions at Highbury. The match was abandoned after 48 minutes.

FRIDAY 10TH DECEMBER 1880

Wednesday legend Andrew Wilson was born in the small Scottish village of Lendalfoot, Ayrshire. He joined the Owls from Clyde for £200 in May 1900 and set a club record of 546 appearances in twenty years at Hillsborough.

SATURDAY 10TH DECEMBER 1960

Two goals apiece from Bobby Lodge and Bobby Craig helped to put Wednesday 5-1 ahead at the interval against Blackburn Rovers. However, a few nerves would have been shredded both on and off the pitch in the second half as Rovers scored three times to leave the Owls hanging on at the death to secure a 5-4 win.

SATURDAY 10TH DECEMBER 1983

The clash of the Second Division promotion rivals Manchester City and Wednesday attracted a 41,862 crowd to Maine Road. City led at the break but the Owls stormed back with a double from Imre Varadi securing a 2-1 win.

THURSDAY 11TH DECEMBER 1947

Pre First World War half-back Bob Ferrier died in Scotland. After retiring from football he had taken employment as a boilermaker in the shipbuilding industry while his son – also called Bob Ferrier – made a club record 626 appearances for Motherwell, netting over 200 goals.

SATURDAY 11TH DECEMBER 1999

In an experiment by the FA, the third round of the FA Cup was played in early December, instead of the usual first Saturday in January. The idea was soon scrapped as only 11,644 were at Hillsborough to see Wednesday scramble past Second Division Bristol City, Andy Booth heading in the only goal after 24 minutes.

SATURDAY 12TH DECEMBER 1953

Despite recovering from a two-goal deficit, Wednesday lost 3-2 at Manchester City and also lost defender Ralph O'Donnell with a broken leg after he collided with City's German goalie Bert Trautmann at a corner, with just three minutes left to play.

FRIDAY 12TH DECEMBER 1986

The Queen officially opened the new covered Kop at Hillsborough. A crowd of 40,000 attended the official ribbon cutting of the new structure.

WEDNESDAY 12TH DECEMBER 1990

The emerging Wednesday side moulded by Ron Atkinson really came to national attention when John Harkes netted a stunning long range effort past Peter Shilton in a 2-1 League Cup replay win at top flight Derby County, sending the Owls into the last eight.

WEDNESDAY 12TH DECEMBER 2000

On a rain soaked pitch at St. Andrew's, the Owls tumbled out of the League Cup at the quarter-final stage, losing 2-0 to Birmingham City with former Owl Danny Sonner netting for the home side.

WEDNESDAY 12TH DECEMBER 2007

The club announced a partnership with Brisbane-based Total Football Academy, run by ex-Owl Adem Poric. The Australian midfielder appeared in 17 games for Wednesday in the 1990s during a five-year stay in Sheffield.

TUESDAY 13TH DECEMBER 1887

One of the greatest goalscorers in the club's history, David Prophet McLean, was born in Forfar, Scotland. After rising to prominence in his homeland he played for Celtic in the infamous 1909 Scottish Cup final replay, which was abandoned due to a riot with the SFA withholding the cup.

SATURDAY 13TH DECEMBER 1924

Wednesday centre-forward Jimmy Trotter scored all five goals as Portsmouth were beaten 5-2 at Hillsborough. The prolific attacker put the Owls 3-2 ahead after 62 minutes and added two more goals in the final 15 minutes to complete the victory, watched by a crowd of 17,255.

SATURDAY 13TH DECEMBER 1930

The Owls thrashed Birmingham City to register their best ever win in league football. A hat-trick from Mark Hooper, braces from Jimmy Seed and Jack Ball plus strikes from Harry Burgess and Ellis Rimmer completed a 9-1 win in front of 21,226 at Hillsborough.

WEDNESDAY 13TH DECEMBER 1961

Despite an own goal from Peter Swan handing AS Roma a 1-0 win in Italy, the Owls progressed through to the next round of the Fairs Cup, winning 4-1 on aggregate.

SATURDAY 14TH DECEMBER 1907

A tram breakdown in the city contributed to a crowd of only 2,000 at Hillsborough to see Wednesday beat Bolton Wanderers 5-2. The fans that could not reach the ground missed a comeback from Wednesday as they trailed by two goals at the interval but registered second-half goals from Jimmy Stewart 2 (59, 69), Frank Bradshaw (79), Tom Brittleton (81) and Andrew Wilson (85).

SATURDAY 14TH DECEMBER 1968

A terrific 4-0 Hillsborough win over Queens Park Rangers kept the Owls in the First Division's top ten. A 22,004 crowd saw goals from Vic Mobley, John Fantham, David Ford and Jim McCalliog complete the biggest win of the 1968/69 campaign.

MONDAY 15TH DECEMBER 1890

Wednesday and Sheffield United met for the first time and 10,000 fans packed into Olive Grove to see goals from Harry Woolhouse and Harry Winterbottom secure a 2-1 win for the Owls, in the friendly meeting.

SATURDAY 15TH DECEMBER 2001

A Gerald Sibon penalty put the Owls level at Gillingham after 23 minutes but the Kent side netted soon after to win 2-1, leaving Wednesday at the wrong end of the First Division table.

SATURDAY 16TH DECEMBER 1995

Yorkshire rivals Leeds United were beaten 6-2 at Hillsborough in a top flight game. Goals from Marc Degryse (2), David Hirst (2), Guy Whittingham and Mark Bright sealed another entertaining game with Hillsborough having witnessed 15 goals in two home games!

SATURDAY 16TH DECEMBER 2000

The two Sheffield teams drew 1-1 at Bramall Lane, in a game televised live by Sky TV. Defender Ian Hendon was an unlikely scorer for the Owls while there was only one offside in the whole game.

SATURDAY 17TH DECEMBER 1960

Future England boss Bobby Robson missed a first-half penalty at The Hawthorns as West Bromwich Albion and Wednesday played out a 2-2 top-flight draw, watched by 17,862.

WEDNESDAY 17TH DECEMBER 1969

It was busy day in the transfer market for Owls boss Danny Williams as he paid £4,000 to non-league Oswestry Town for Eric Potts and signed Harold Wilcockson from Doncaster Rovers, sending Ian Branfoot and Archie Irvine to Donny in exchange.

SATURDAY 18TH DECEMBER 1880

Wednesday won 4-0 at Blackburn Rovers in their first ever FA Cup game. A hat-trick from Bob Gregory and a goal from Harry Winterbottom secured a place in the third round.

SATURDAY 18TH DECEMBER 1937

In farcical conditions, Burnley and Wednesday drew 1-1 at Turf Moor on a pitch that was covered with two inches of snow and a layer of ice. Incredibly before the game the referee had used a hammer to test the pitch and duly gave the go ahead!

SATURDAY 18TH DECEMBER 1993

In what has become known as 'Waddle's game', the former England international produced a second-half masterclass that inspired Wednesday to a 5-0 win over West Ham United at Hillsborough. He turned visiting full-back David Burrows into a quivering wreck, leaving the poor defender on his behind after one dazzling run!

WEDNESDAY 19TH DECEMBER 2001

An astonishing solo goal from Matt Hamshaw was the highlight as Wednesday beat fellow First Division side, Watford, 4-0 at Hillsborough to reach the semi-finals of the League Cup. Hamshaw's 70-yard run had put the Owls 2-0 ahead while goals in the final two minutes from Phil O'Donnell and Trond Soltvedt completed a great night for the majority in a 20,319 crowd.

SUNDAY 19TH DECEMBER 2004

Steve MacLean became the first Wednesday player to score a league hat-trick away from home since February 1972 as he grabbed a treble in the 4-0 win over Doncaster Rovers at Belle Vue.

SATURDAY 20TH DECEMBER 1924

A hat-trick from Hull City centre-forward Paddy Mills sent the Owls to a 4-2 Second Division defeat at City's old Analby Road ground. The game also marked the final appearance of long-serving keeper Teddy Davison who was subsequently kept out of the side by Jack Brown before signing for Mansfield Town in June 1926.

SATURDAY 20TH DECEMBER 1952

The Geordie fans in the 37,927 crowd were left stunned as Wednesday won 5-1 at Newcastle United, Derek Dooley (2), Jackie Sewell (2) and Jackie Marriott netting for the Owls in the top flight game.

FRIDAY 20TH DECEMBER 1974

Fans' favourite Tommy Craig left for Newcastle United – Wednesday receiving a club record transfer fee of £120,000 from the north-east club. He departed after 233 games for the Owls, over five years, after joining as a raw 18-year-old in May 1969. He later played at Aston Villa and Carlisle United before being appointed player-coach at Edinburgh club Hibernian. He then spent eight years on the coaching staff at Newcastle United before joining Belgian side Charleroi as assistant to John Collins in December 2008.

WEDNESDAY 21ST DECEMBER 1938

Wednesday players Bill Fallon and Ted Catlin were hospitalised after the car they were travelling in skidded on a snowy Penistone Road and careered into a telegraph pole!

SATURDAY 21ST DECEMBER 1957

In a fluctuating game at Hillsborough, visitors Manchester City left with the two points after a 5-4 victory. The Owls had recovered from being two goals down at one stage to level the scores at 4-4 but City scored the winner through Bobby Johnstone with six minutes remaining to leave Wednesday just one place off the bottom rung in the First Division.

THURSDAY 21ST DECEMBER 1967

Pre First World War attacker 'Davie' McLean died back in his hometown of Forfar, eight days after celebrating his 80th birthday. After retiring from the game, following various coaching roles, he was somewhat of a local celebrity and regularly watched his local side Forfar Athletic until his passing.

SATURDAY 21ST DECEMBER 2002

Wednesday slipped to the bottom of the Championship table as Grimsby Town won 2-0 in Cleethorpes. A wrretched display meant the Owls faced a desperate fight against relegation in the New Year.

SATURDAY 22ND DECEMBER 1889

Wednesday recorded their second 9-1 home win of the 1889/90 season with Billy Ingram scoring five, and Mickey Bennett four, as Small Heath (Birmingham City) were put to the sword.

1970S OWLS MIDFIELDER TOMMY CRAIG (RIGHT) WITH FORMER SCOTLAND BOSS CRAIG BROWN

SATURDAY 22ND DECEMBER 1923

Centre-forward Sid Binks scored four times as Crystal Palace were beaten 6-0 at Hillsborough in a Second Division fixture, to continue their unbeaten home record. The north-east born centre-forward netted after 5, 43, 60 and 68 minutes and would also grab two hat-tricks during his spell at Wednesday. He'd won back-to-back FA Amateur Cups with Bishop Auckland in the early 1920s and represented England at amateur level before turning professional with the Owls in 1922.

SATURDAY 22ND DECEMBER 1951

With Derek Dooley virtually unstoppable the Owls beat Everton 4-0 at Hillsborough with the big number nine scoring all four, all his goals hitting the net in the second half. A crowd of 38,986 fans were inside Hillsborough to see the phenomenon that was Dooley score his third hat-trick of the season and take Wednesday to top spot in the Second Division for the first time in the season. The goals from Dooley also set a record that has never been bettered – it meant he had scored in NINE consecutive league games.

SATURDAY 23RD DECEMBER 1933

A goal from Harry Burgess, after 11 minutes, clinched a 1-0 win at the Victoria Ground, Stoke. The top flight game marked the end of Jack Ball's Wednesday career – he was controversially replaced by Neil Dewar who joined from Manchester United six days later in a swap deal that took Ball to Old Trafford.

SATURDAY 23RD DECEMBER 1978

The Third Division home game with Hull City was one of four home matches postponed at Hillsborough during the 1978/79 season; Blackpool, Brentford and Mansfield Town also falling to the good old British winter.

SATURDAY 23RD DECEMBER 2006

History was made at Hillsborough as loan goalkeeper Mark Crossley became the first Wednesday custodian to score in open play. With the Owls trailing 3-2 to visitors Southampton, and with three minutes of added time already having been played, Crossley ran to the Kop end and duly headed home from Chris Brunt's corner to start huge scenes of celebration both on and off the pitch!

SATURDAY 24TH DECEMBER 1927

In front of only 12,345 fans at Villa Park, the home side and Wednesday were involved in a nine-goal thriller with Aston Villa winning 5-4. The Owls led 3-1 after just 20 minutes but it was 4-3 to Villa by the interval with Joe Beresford scoring three. A late goal from Jimmy Seed provided mere consolation as Wednesday remained near the foot of the First Division.

TUESDAY 24TH DECEMBER 1957

After 17 goals in 83 games, winger Albert Broadbent moved to Rotherham United in part-exchange for Peter Johnson. Wednesday also paid the Millers £6,000 with Johnson becoming the club's automatic choice at right-back during the early 1960s.

MONDAY 24TH DECEMBER 1973

Wednesday controversially sacked manager Derek Dooley with the side hovering around the relegation zone after a season blighted by injuries and illness. The former goalscoring legend did not return to Hillsborough for almost 20 years, with chairman Matt Sheppard forever associated with the somewhat callous dismissal.

TUESDAY 25TH DECEMBER 1917

The horrors of the First World War were temporarily put aside as 35,000 fans attended the Sheffield derby game at Bramall Lane in a Midland Section match. A seventh-minute goal from Kitchen won the game for the Blades.

MONDAY 25TH DECEMBER 1950

The Owls' struggles at the bottom of the First Division received a boost on this day as goals from Johnny Jordan, Hugh McJarrow and Red Froggatt earned a 3-1 win at West Bromwich Albion. Despite the two points the club remained bottom of the league.

WEDNESDAY 25TH DECEMBER 1957

A crowd of 26,825 watched what proved to be the last Christmas Day game played at Hillsborough as Wednesday and Preston North End shared eight goals. Alan Finney scored twice for the Owls who led 3-1 at one stage before needing a Derek Wilkinson strike to salvage a point.

TUESDAY 26th DECEMBER 1905

A Boxing Day crowd of 18,000 watched as Wednesday beat bottom club Wolverhampton Wanderers 5-1 at Hillsborough with Jimmy Stewart becoming the first Owls player to score four times in the top flight.

TUESDAY 26th DECEMBER 1911

In an incredible game at Hillsborough, the Owls raced into a 7-0 lead at half-time against Sunderland. Centre-forward David McLean scored a thirteen-minute hat-trick before the break and added a fourth goal to his personal tally in the second half to complete an 8-0 rout.

WEDNESDAY 26th DECEMBER 1923

Wednesday beat Coventry City 2-0 at Hillsborough on a snow-covered pitch. In fact, conditions were so bad that the Owls painted the goalposts dark blue!

FRIDAY 26th DECEMBER 1947

A crowd of 37,343 were at Hillsborough for the visit of West Ham United and saw Eddie Quigley grab four goals, including a first-half treble, as the Londoners were beaten 5-3. Born in Bury in July 1921, Quigley scored 52 goals in just 78 appearances for the club and the British transfer record was broken in December 1949 when he was sold to Preston North End for £26,000.

FRIDAY 26th DECEMBER 1958

Lincoln City were put to the sword at Hillsborough as league leaders Wednesday won 7-0 with 'Red' Froggatt, Roy Shiner and John Fantham all scoring two goals each.

MONDAY 26th DECEMBER 1960

Tragedy struck on the way home from the game at Arsenal as the team coach skidded off the A1 near Huntingdon, trapping 19-year-old reserve player Doug McMillan in the wreckage. Sadly for the Scot, the attending medical team had no option but to amputate his right leg, just below the knee, so he could be pulled clear of the mangled coach. He became the second Wednesday player in just over eight years to have his career ended in such tragic circumstances.

SATURDAY 26TH DECEMBER 1970

In a Second Division game at Hull City, the Owls led 4-1 with seven minutes remaining but unbelievably went back to Sheffield with only a point after the Tigers scored three times in the remaining time to force an unlikely 4-4 draw.

WEDNESDAY 26TH DECEMBER 1979

The Owls set a divisional crowd record of 49,309 as neighbours United were beaten 4-0 in a game subsequently referred to by Wednesday fans as 'The Boxing Day massacre'. An Ian Mellor goal after 39 minutes put Wednesday on their way and further strikes from Terry Curran (62), Jeff King (64) and a Mark Smith penalty (86) completed the scoring.

SATURDAY 26TH DECEMBER 1992

In a breathtaking game at Hillsborough, watched by 37,708, the Owls led champions elect Manchester United 3-0 thanks to goals from David Hirst, Mark Bright and John Sheridan. However, the Red Devils stormed back to draw 3-3 with Brian McClair (2) and Eric Cantona on the scoresheet.

FRIDAY 26TH DECEMBER 2003

The Owls lost 3-2 at home to Port Vale in a Second Division game while club legend Redfern Froggatt died in Sheffield, aged 79. His tally of 148 senior goals makes 'Red' the third most prolific goalscorer in Wednesday's history.

FRIDAY 27TH DECEMBER 1872

One of the greatest captains in Owls history was born in Sheffield. Tommy Crawshaw won twelve full caps for England and in a fourteen-year stay with Wednesday scored 26 times in 465 appearances.

THURSDAY 27TH DECEMBER 1934

Jack Surtees was signed after a hugely successful trial period. He was so despondent about football, after being released by Northampton Town, that he booked a passage to America to start a new life. However, his brother persuaded Owls boss Billy Walker to give him a trial and inside six months Surtees was playing at Wembley as Wednesday won the FA Cup!

MONDAY 28th DECEMBER 1891

A bumper crowd of 10,000 packed into Olive Grove to see Wednesday win 7-2 against Lincoln City in an Alliance League fixture.

MONDAY 28th DECEMBER 1896

A hat-trick from Bob Ferrier helped Wednesday ease the pain of a Boxing Day defeat at Bramall Lane as Blackburn Rovers were beaten 6-0, Alec Brady, Archie Brash and a Porter own goal completing the scoring.

MONDAY 28th DECEMBER 1908

On a frostbound Owlerton pitch, Wednesday adapted better to conditions than their visitors Woolwich Arsenal to register a 6-2 win; an Andrew Wilson treble helped to seal the points as Wednesday retained fourth place in the First Division. Only 8,000 were inside the ground with weather conditions a contributory factor.

SATURDAY 28th DECEMBER 1974

An Eric Potts goal after just three minutes was enough for Wednesday to take the points from their visit to Southampton. Sadly though, in that desperate 1974/75 campaign, the win would be the club's last of the season, Wednesday losing 14 of the final 17 games!

MONDAY 29th DECEMBER 1890

Lancashire club Darwen were beaten 7-3 at Olive Grove in an Alliance League fixture. Hat-tricks from both Albert Mumford and 'Toddles' Woolhouse secured the win in a rare high point of a season where the club finished rock bottom of the Alliance League.

SATURDAY 29th DECEMBER 1984

A brace from Lee Chapman and a goal from Imre Varadi took the Owls to a resounding 3-0 win at The Dell, against Southampton. The points left Wednesday sixth in the First Division.

WEDNESDAY 29th DECEMBER 1999

Wednesday and Chelsea met at Stamford Bridge in the final top flight game of the twentieth century. It was a sign of the times that the London side did not contain one English player in their starting eleven; the multinational Pensioners winning 3-0, leaving the Owls bottom of the league.

ACTION FROM CHELSEA V WEDNESDAY – THE FINAL TOP FLIGHT GAME OF THE 20TH CENTURY

SATURDAY 30TH DECEMBER 1893

For the third time in the 1893/94 season, Wednesday were involved in an abandoned league game. After snow, mud and rain had claimed the first two, it was dense fog at Olive Grove which caused the game with Darwen to be halted after 58 minutes with the score tied at 2-2.

SUNDAY 30TH DECEMBER 1923

Reserve team player Tom Armitage died in hospital, aged just 24, five days after being severely injured in the Christmas Day second-team game against Rotherham Town. His brother, Len, had made three appearances for Wednesday in the first season after the Great War.

SATURDAY 30TH DECEMBER 2000

The Owls drew 0-0 at Huddersfield Town in a First Division derby at the McAlpine Stadium. Wednesday finished the match with only ten men after Gerald Sibon was booked twice in the 76th minute, resulting in an early bath and palpable frustration for boss Paul Jewell.

TUESDAY 31ST DECEMBER 1907

Wednesday moved up into second place in the First Division after thrashing Woolwich Arsenal 6-0 at Owlerton. A hat-trick from Frank Bradshaw and goals from Andrew Wilson, Tom Brittleton and Harry Chapman kept up the title challenge.

SATURDAY 31ST DECEMBER 1932

In a New Year's Eve thriller at Blackpool, the Owls recovered from 2-0 behind to win 4-3, Alf Strange, Ron Starling, Harry Burgess and Ellis Rimmer netting in a victory that left Wednesday third in the First Division.

SATURDAY 31ST DECEMBER 1966

A crowd of 31,032 were inside Hillsborough to see the Owls beat Chelsea 6-1 in a top flight encounter. Doubles from John Ritchie and David Ford, plus strikes from Jim McCalliog and John Fantham, helped Wednesday to see out the old year in fine style.

BIBLIOGRAPHY

Sheffield Wednesday A Complete Record 1867-1987
Keith Farnsworth
Breedon Books

100 Years at Hillsborough
Jason Dickinson
Hallamshire Press

The Wednesday Boys
A Who's Who of Sheffield Wednesday 1880-2005
John Brodie and Jason Dickinson
Pickard Communication

Rothmans/Sky Sports Yearbooks (1970-2008)
Jack Rollin
Headline

www.guardian.co.uk